Teaching Children Through

NATURAL MATHEMATICS

Robert
C.
Dwyer

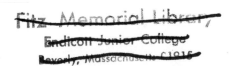

Jane
K.
Elligett

Parker Publishing Co., Inc.   West Nyack, New York

Dedicated

to

JOHN DEWEY

A Word from the Authors
About This Book

The authors believe that Natural Mathematics will assist the teacher in providing successful educational experiences for her pupils, with more satisfaction to them and to her, and with more continuing benefits for their further progress. Natural Mathematics presents specific teaching procedures designed to enable the child to solve problems, acquire skills, and develop concepts. The nature of these procedures will maximize the child's ability to transfer learning, and to use present learning as a foundation for cumulative academic achievement.

The teacher will find the procedures of Natural Mathematics useful as a developmental program for children of all abilities and backgrounds. Since the program is a developmental one, it should be used in the sequential progression of the child's learning. But it is similarly effective in its remedial application by enabling the teacher to locate the child's learning difficulty and provide him with a foundation and a regression level. We believe that the teacher will find Natural Mathematics a particularly gratifying approach to teaching those children who do not respond to current practices, even when such practices are repeated many times or modified in many ways. Natural Mathematics provides the teacher with a sequential program which she may use exclusively, or for a part of each day. The more she uses it developmentally, that is, as a program to *develop* the child as a learner, the less frequently it will be needed as a means of rectifying learning problems.

The teacher will find that the approaches and procedures of Natural Mathematics are designed to conform to the child's natural motivation. Natural Mathematics thus relieves the teacher of the frustrating and unproductive burden of opposing the child's immediate concerns. Instead of apologist for academic learning, the teacher becomes a director of child-centered events in which academic learning emerges as a natural means for the child to reach his own goals. The teacher's role—as one who explains, requires, and prohibits—is transformed to one who designs, provides, mediates, and reviews.

In the development of Natural Mathematics, the authors have regarded the child's inherent motivation to act as the source of his learning potential. Natural Mathematics provides for the media of action (the tools and strategies) in their natural developmental sequence in the child's construction of reality. The child's learning potential is most efficiently cultivated, however, when he is faced with two problems simultaneously: an immediate problem at hand, as well as the ongoing and cumulative problem of devising more adequate tools and strategies. The ongoing problem leads to the development of more sophisticated procedures, but only if the immediate problem mobilizes the child. Natural Mathematics, therefore, includes developmental learning experiences, or "events," in which academic learning is integrated with the child's choices of behavior, appropriate to his level.

The goal is the child's mastery of the most refined medium, the use of symbols. The central principle of Natural Mathematics is that the child will not master symbolic strategy unless he discovers it developmentally. This book is thus dedicated to the proposition that the *manner* in which a child learns is of crucial importance if he is to become an independent learner. (The authors would suggest that there is a form of integrity in *not* learning, if it is a resistance to the irrelevant. Such resistance is itself an intelligent act.)

A child must first trust his perceptions before he can begin to formulate his concepts. He comes to trust his perceptions through acts of verification. We hold that a child's loyalty to this procedure is sovereign. The critical test of our respect is that we allow the child to do the verifying in terms of *his* perceptions and *his* criteria of meaning. That is, we will truly be respecting the child's loyalty to his own verification, when we value the kinds of things he would do if "left on his own."

We will acknowledge that the child does not construct reality with any deliberate motive to construct it objectively.

The educational challenge is thus to make the activities in the classroom natural, by giving them the structure that a child in less artificial surroundings would give them himself. Such activities would be relevant to the child's immediate interests, would integrate many of the child's adaptive abilities simultaneously (perception, cognition, memory, motivation), and would focus on a child-centered problem in which subject matter was not fragmented. When these are provided, we maintain that a child can learn faster and better than a teacher can "teach," that no amount of "teaching" can match a child's learning potential when a teacher thus releases it.

The teacher's irreplaceable contribution is in providing a medium by which the child's motivational system can join his perceptual and cognitive system. When the teacher has presented the child with a structured sequence of events, which demand the child's integration of his perceptions and cognition in the action of problem-solving, and which provide for the repetition and variation necessary for strategy development, the teacher has set the stage for the miracle of learning.

Several recent recommendations for the future direction of education suggest that a child should be taught all the "basic skills" in the most intensive manner, when he is very young. It is suggested that sophisticated teaching devices are able to accomplish this efficiently. Once this has been achieved, it is suggested that the child and teacher are then free to enter what is considered to be the "creative" aspects of learning. The authors of Natural Mathematics feel that this is a misguided notion, and is an application of the traditional and current convention that skills and concepts should be learned first, and in isolation, and then applied later to problems. However, by merely making these problems more interesting and more creative, one does not compensate for the early fragmentation of a child's natural, creative, integrated approach to learning and reality. If the young child is force-fed symbolic skills (assuming that it is possible), the child's judgment is focused on language, rather than on the reality which language describes. If his creativity is not stifled in the process, it may be channeled into "dilettante-ism" or mere precociousness.

The theories and procedures of Natural Mathematics have grown out of the authors' many years of teaching children of all abilities and all ages. The authors' basic premises have been influenced by the principles and work of Dewey and Piaget. The Hierarchies of Natural Mathematics develop these principles into a teaching model, which the authors believe has been lacking heretofore.

For this reason, this book is especially addressed to teachers who have felt that a breakdown occurs somewhere between the accepted teaching principles and the classroom programs which are intended to implement them. These teachers have been frustrated because it seems that the what-to-do and what-to-say in these programs "ought" to involve the child's potential, but somehow it often does not. They have occasionally despaired because the rationality of the approach does not elicit the expected rational response from the pupil. They are discouraged when the transfer which is built into the programs is not carried over into transfer by the child.

It is hoped that the teaching model of Natural Mathematics will provide them, and all teachers, with a means of bringing theory and practice closer together.

Acknowledgments

The authors wish to express their particular appreciation to the following people for their assistance in field work testing and the collection of data:

Shirley West
Mrs. Mary Anne Brost
Mrs. Carol Patterson
Mrs. Lola Allen
Mrs. Louise Schoenborn
Mrs. LaVerne Wingate

In addition, the authors are especially grateful to Mrs. Elizabeth Schmidt for her patience and understanding during the numerous revisions.

Contents

The Basic Flaw in Traditional Approaches, "Old" or
"New" · Ten Major Principles of Natural Mathematics
Frequently Violated by Current Procedures · Transfer,
Intuition and Motivation · The Reason for the Present
Dilemma

From Distributing (Matching) Real Objects to Com-
puting with Symbols · A Step-by-Step Progression from
the Concrete to the Abstract · The Intermediate Repre-
sentations of the Objects and of the Actions · The Use of
Symbols and Computations as Short-Cuts for Solutions
Already Discovered · An Outline of the Media-Action
Hierarchy · Phases I to VI—Sample Problem-Solution in
Each Phase

How Children Learn to Identify with Problems—
From the Hedonistic and Egocentric to the Impersonal
and Objective · An Outline of the Role-Playing Hierarchy · The Continuing Importance of the Real, for Regression and Reference

Emphasis on the Development of the Child's Rational
Structure Rather Than Development of Mathematical
Structure · Exercises Versus Problems · Five Prerequisites
of a Problem · Three Principles of Complexity of Problem
Hierarchy · Summary of Problem-Solving Hierarchies · A
New Way of Identifying Not Only What-Is-the-Matter,
But What-to-Do · A Diagnostic Profile of a Child's Per-
formance Pattern on Two Problems

A Case Against Early Introduction of Sets · Analysis
of the Violation of the Child's Natural Concerns

An Early Sample Event in Natural Mathematics ·
Comparison with Traditional Lessons · Suggestions for
More Complex Variations · Sharing as an Introduction to
Fractions

PART 1

Presentation and Analysis
of
Natural Mathematics

PROLOGUE

A Teacher's Story

I teach a fifth grade class in a slum-area school.

Joe comes to school each morning without breakfast. Some days he doesn't come to school because he is tired, or decides to wait for his mother to come home. He may not have seen her since the previous day. She does domestic day-work irregularly, coming and going at different times. Some nights she does not come home. His grandmother lives in the house. She takes care of his two younger sisters and the baby. The woman next door sometimes leaves her two young children with them also. Sometimes the grandmother takes the baby, and has Joe stay home with the sisters. Joe does not know his father. Sometimes a man comes to the house at night with his mother. The sisters are put in Joe's bed. Joe's mother and grandmother fight a lot. The grandmother gets drunk once in a while. Joe's mother gets angry when he stays home from school, but she does not stay angry with him. She almost always brings groceries home and has some money left over. Nearly always she gives him a dime or a quarter. She tells him he should go to school every day, and get smart so that he can be a big man. She tells him to do what the teacher says, and above all, to stay out of trouble. Joe has never been in trouble, but he steals when he can, and he thinks about stealing in his daydreams.

Julieann's father lives at home. He works several days a week on construction jobs. The days he does not work, he sleeps late. He is usually gone when the children get home. He has a violent temper and when he is angry, he sometimes beats Julieann with a belt. The children avoid him. Julieann's mother frequently has bruises from fights which Julieann hears from her bed. Julieann's mother has a regular job in a laundry. She leaves in the morning before the children are awake, but she is home almost every night by 6:00. She fixes supper for whoever is there, and goes to sleep on the sofa. She cries a lot, complains of backache constantly. When Julieann's 15 year old brother comes in, she accuses him of being late, tells him that he doesn't know how hard she works, and cries again.

Julieann watches television, thinks about boys, and studies the way the older girls behave.

Most of my pupils come from families like Joe's and Julieann's. These pupils are mostly 10 and 11 years old; some are 12 and 13. They have twelve years of public education available to them. I feel that many of them have lost out already. Most range from second to fourth grade achievement in language arts and arithmetic; they slip further behind each year; they will not, or cannot, concentrate on their work. They have active minds, but they do not do the kind of thinking necessary for academic success. In many there is a courteous kind of withdrawal; they look at me, but they don't listen; they open their books, but they don't read; they get out pencil and paper, but they don't write. Some of the older ones are beginning to refuse even these forms of cooperation. Sometimes I feel that school is driving these children away from the social and academic goals of education, instead of bringing them toward these goals—out of society, not into it.

I am a certified teacher, with eight years of classroom experience. I am considered to have good classroom control. I believe that I am flexible, patient, and genuinely sympathetic. I have attended summer institutes and workshops, and I read the professional journals. I am aware of learning theory, know that children must be taught at their readiness level, must be motivated, and must be brought from the concrete to the abstract. I am exhausted from trying to be and do these things effectively; I am in despair because I have so little success to match against so much failure; I am frustrated because the sources of professional help have not given me a method which reaches these children. I am now beginning to doubt myself and to suspect that perhaps I am not competent.

Last week, at the beginning of the term, I again resolved to go "all the way" with an adopted text. I have made this resolution many times. Always, at some point, so many children are lost, that I abandon the text and go back to plain, old-fashioned blackboard explanation and drill. When this in turn fails, I regret that I gave up so soon. This time, I am determined that I will not give up, no matter what. I am to begin teaching the addition of fractions.

Although the children are in the fifth grade, I decide to run dittoes of a lesson from a fourth grade book. I know that the children have had those lessons the previous year. Several sources suggest that the number line will help the child learn to add fractions, and that fractions should be called rational numbers. I almost give up before I start, since I suspect that most of the children cannot make a number line. They will not mark off the integers at equal intervals. I suspect that they are even less able to make a number line showing the fractions. However, I can show the fraction number lines for each exercise, with the arrows showing the jumps on several sample exercises. (I am also braced for a blank response to the word "rational." But I am aware that it is mathematically sounder than "fraction"—and I am determined. I recognize the early signs of giving up, and resist them.)

I draw a number line on the board, label the points 0,1,2,3, and then divide each segment of this number line into fourths. I realize that I should have the children assist me in labeling these points starting with 0/4, 1/4, etc. This I cannot do. There is not one child in the class capable of it. I do the next best thing. I have one of the best pupils come to the board, and tell her exactly what to write and where. I find that I must write the numerals off to the side, so that she can copy them. She cannot write the numeral symbol for the words "five-fourths." I observe with apprehension that half the children in the class are no longer watching.

One guide suggests that I now cross out or cover up the whole numbers to avoid the problem of mixed numerals. My sense of humor rescues me: the whole numbers are the only numerals my class relates to at all. But this gives me the chance to call another pupil to the board to use the eraser and to recapture the children's attention. We have been 10 minutes coming to this point, and my children's attention span is spent. We have not yet begun the lesson, and restlessness has become general. I decide to call a drink-and-talk break, and select five children to draw fraction number lines on the board in colored chalk.

We return to the lesson, and I tell the children that they are going to investigate addition of rational numbers on the number line in the same way they add whole numbers on the number line. I ask a pupil how much is 2 plus 4, hastily draw a whole-number line, and show the jumps to 6. I know that I must take the time for this review in order to keep the children with me at all. It flashes across my mind that the number line is not teaching addition; addition is teaching the number line.

I now draw an arrow from 0/4 to 2/4 and another arrow from 2/4 to 6/4, and write the corresponding equation $2/4 + 4/4 = 6/4$. At this time, the children are engaged in a variety of activities, mostly peaceful, but also inattentive and distracting. I need to restore order and a common focus of attention. I instruct everybody to take out pencil and paper and we will all do this together on lesson sheets which I now pass out. At this point, I want very badly to give up. I know that this is the wrong approach. I already am certain that I will go all the way back to Book 1 if necessary, tomorrow. I know that these children can learn, and that this is not teaching them. But I have been in this vicious cycle before, and this time I am going to exhaust this particular possibility.

I tell the children that they are to listen and watch what I do at the board, and then copy it down exactly on their paper. I repeat the boardwork exactly as before:

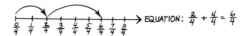

I pass out the exercise sheets, and instruct the class to do the exercises while I walk by and check what they have copied from the board. Out of 30 children, roughly 10 have not copied anything from the board, 10 have tried but their arrows terminate at the wrong points, 10 have copied the number line and the arrows correctly, but only 2 have also copied the equation without an error. The children who did not copy the example from the board, of course, are not doing the exercises either. I get to as many as I can; I take their hand in mine and begin moving their pencil for them. I stay right by them and direct them while they draw the number line for the first exercise, draw the arrows, mark off the fourths, and enter the numbers. I ask each of these children to copy this over, right underneath, by himself. I only get to 4 children in ten minutes. Except for 4 or 5, the others have abandoned the exercise. They are giggling, whispering, sharpening pencils, asking if they can go to the restroom, and some of the boys are chewing paper.

I ask that the papers be passed forward, and call for reading groups.

That night I look over the papers.

Exercise 1 was to write the addition equation for the following number-line picture:

The correct equation is, of course, 1/4 + 2/4 = 3/4.

The equations on the children's papers include "1 + 2 = 3," "1 + 3 = 4," "1/4 + 3/4 = 3/4," "1/4, 3/4," "0/4 + 1/4 = 3/4."

The conceptual difficulty is, of course, that the pupils don't know what a fraction is. I am confirmed in my opinion that the fourth grade lesson was too advanced, too abstract; but I feel justified, because I did go all the way with it.

I refer back to some introductory lessons on fractions at the third grade level. Many of these use pictures to illustrate fractions, for instance, a circle half shaded in red, a square half shaded in red, 8 triangles with 4 shaded in red. Similar groups of pictures illustrate 1/3. The exercises will consist of similar pictures, partly shaded; the pupils are to write whether 1/2 or 1/3 is shaded. I am worried about the type of picture in which several items of a set are shaded, rather than a part of a single figure. To the children, these are two different matters.

I make up a master of such figures and run off copies. I also make a master of some unmarked circles, rectangles, and triangles which the children can divide and shade themselves.

The next day, I pass these out first. I demonstrate 1/2 and 1/3 on the flannel board, by putting up two half-pies and three third-pies. Then, at the board, I draw a circle and draw a line through the center. I ask the children to do the same thing with one of their circles. I shade 1/2 of my circle; I ask the children to shade 1/2 of theirs. I write 1/2 inside both half circles, and ask them to do the same. I explain that I have divided the circle into 2 parts, and that each part is called 1/2, that this means 1 of the 2 parts.

I now ask the children to divide the rest of the figures in the first row in half, shade one-half with their red pencils, and write 1/2 on each part. While I have been instructing them, several children have started reaching under their seats for pencils; some have gotten up into the aisle and are bending over, hunting. Books, notebooks, purses and pencils slide onto the floor. Some cannot find their red pencils. I give out some extras that I have and tell the rest to shade in lead pencil. A few are still asking around if they can borrow. One pupil asks if he can use a lot of colors. I explain that any color will be all right, providing they only color one-half of each figure.

I realize that I am teaching a second grade lesson, but that is irrelevant. If this is the level of the pupils' capability, this is what they should be doing. Most of the children are happy and some of them are doing the work, and correctly. But some of the children are not. Two boys are snatching each other's papers back and forth across the aisle. I go over to them, tell them that's not the way to behave, smooth out their papers. One of the papers has a dirty word written on it. I tear it up and replace it with a new sheet. I look at him severely; then indicate with my finger the line he is to draw through the first figure. The other boy asks for a new sheet too. I give it to him. Both boys do not know what to do. I explain again, and tell the rest of the class that whoever has done the first row should go on and do the rest. I reach across the aisle for a paper which has the first row done correctly and neatly, and hold it up for everyone to see. I remind the class that the papers don't have to be the same, that you can divide something in half with a line going across, or up and down, or diagonally from one corner to another.

Again I get to as many individually as I can, and after fifteen minutes have the papers passed in. Over half the class can do this. However, on several papers, the entire figure was shaded, or the divisions were nowhere near equal. Some children have drawn circles inside the rectangles; some have drawn faces in the circles. A number of pupils have written "1" in each part, but not the "/2" part of the fraction. Some papers have only one or two figures divided; some the first row.

The following day, I repeat the same lesson, but with the division into thirds instead of halves. Many children who were successful with halves cannot do the same thing with thirds. I explain that it is just the same, except that we are going to divide each figure into 3 parts. I repeat the demonstrations, I repeat the board examples. By the end of the lesson, I am getting about the same performance as the previous day.

I decide that the children are still not ready for repetition of the third grade lesson. I will use more concrete materials than pictures of figures; I will use figure cut-outs. The next day, I also bring an apple to class. Before passing out the cut-outs, I cut the apple into halves. I hold up one part of the apple, and ask, "What part of the apple is this?" The response, "One-half," is general. I hold up a paper plate, and ask, "How shall I divide this in half?" Several children say, "Cut it." "Where?" I ask, and cut off about a third. "Is it cut in half?" I ask. Some of the children look uncertain; most say "No." I explain that the whole is cut in half only if both parts are the same size. "Are these two parts the same size?" I ask. The children all say "No." "Then is it cut in half?" I ask again. A larger number of children say, "No." But some of the children who paid attention while I was cutting are no longer watching. I take another paper plate and cut it in half. All agree that it is correct.

I have each pupil take a piece of paper and fold it in half; I tell them to draw a line down the fold; I write 1/2 on the board, and ask the pupils to write 1/2 on each half of their folded paper.

I repeat the paper plate demonstration for thirds.

The flannel board figures, of a pie cut in half and a pie cut in thirds, are still there from the previous day. I have each pupil take another sheet of paper, and try to fold it in thirds. I demonstrate how to get it nearly equally divided by trial and error, how to draw a line along the best folds. I tell them to write 1/3 on each part.

I now pass out rectangle and circle cut-outs, a red pair and a blue pair to each pupil. I ask them to divide the red figures into halves, by drawing a line through them, and the blue ones into thirds, and to write 1/2 or 1/3 on each part. There is much looking around to see what the others are doing, and I repeat the instructions. Several children fold all their fingers into halves. One girl sets hers up on her desk like little tents; one tries to hang his over his ears; a few of the boys try to flick a cut-out across to another desk. I call for order and ask everyone to look at the flannel board as I point to the pie cut in thirds. I ask anyone who has a blue circle divided like this to hold it up. Ten children have one. Five children have 1/3 written on each of the three parts.

I tell the children to put the cut-outs under their seats. It is imperative that they be placed out of reach.

The next day, I concentrate on the meaning of 1/2 of a set. I place 12 rulers on the desk and ask Henry to come up and divide them into 2 equal piles. He almost gets it right, putting 7 in one pile and 5 in the other. Several children correct him; he makes it 6 and 6. He asks me if it is right, now. I assure him that it is. I explain that each pile is 1/2 of the set of 12, just like each pie piece was 1/2 of the whole pie.

I call 10 children to the front of the room. I explain that they are the whole set. I separate them into 2 groups of 5 each. The class counts as I touch each child. I ask what part each group is out of the whole set. Several children call out "5." I explain that each group has 5 children, it is true, but that these 5 make up 1/2 of the whole set because it is 1 part of the 2 parts I have made. Meanwhile, one of the children has dropped something on the floor, gone off after it and sat down. One of the girls from the same group slipped over to join a friend in the other group. One of the boys is entertaining the class with funny faces. The children care about who is at the front of the room, and what they are doing, but they do not care how many.

I have the children return to their seats and I pass out the exercise sheet which shows both figures and sets already shaded. The pupil is to write whether the shaded part is 1/2 or 1/3. Some examples are:

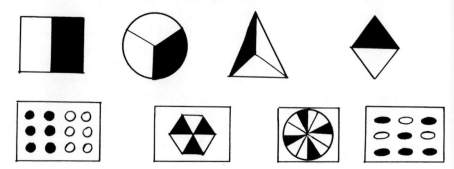

The first row of exercises should no longer present a serious problem. But we are still in difficulty on the others, especially because our experience with dividing sets of rulers and sets of children, etc., clearly separated the rulers or children into "geographic" groups. Many of these pictures do not. I tell the class to think of the shaded figures as one group and the unshaded figures as another. I illustrate several similar exercises at the board and tell the class to begin. During this exercise, I do not walk through the room. Nor do I give help. I want to know what the children can do. I allow 15 minutes and call for the papers.

On checking the papers that evening, I find that only five pupils have done all of the exercises correctly. Out of the 15 exercises, there are only four which were answered correctly by over half the class. These were the single figures.

On the exercise [▨] , the answers were frequently 3, or 9, or 3/6.

On the exercise [✸] , a frequent answer was 4.

I have spent 5 days with my fifth graders, starting with a fourth grade lesson, going back to third grade, then back to first grade, then forward to third. On the first day of the following week, I give the fourth grade exercises over again, and on the next day, an informal test. On looking over the papers, and comparing them with the papers of the week before, there is very little improvement. We had come nowhere near understanding fractions on a number line. We had not worked with any fractions except halves and thirds. We had not looked at any fractions except unit fractions. All this still lies between where my children are, and where they ought to be. And they have been through it all before.

After these discouraging days of work, I also know that the hardest test is still to come. We are building these skills in order to be able to apply them to problems. If pupils can make this application to word problems, we feel assured that they have acquired the concepts and are safe in going on to new skills. Certainly a child can be taught a number of new skills without ever grasping the concepts underlying the earlier ones. But we know that this kind of skill-building does not lead to an understanding of the structure of mathematics. It does not create a growing foundation. Sooner or later, the child simply acquires a bag of tricks which is too large for him to use. He no longer knows which trick to select in order to solve a problem.

I assign the following problems: (1) John has a candy bar. He wants to share it with his two best friends. He wants each of them to have as much as he has. What part of the candy bar will each of them have? (2) Mary has 30 crayons. Sue asks for 1/2 of them. If Mary agrees, how many crayons will she give to Sue? (3) John has read 1/3 of a book. He has just finished page 33. How many pages are in the book?

The distribution of answers follows [1] :

First Problem			Second Problem		
Correct Answer	*Number of Children*		*Correct Answer*	*Number of Children*	
1/3	3		15	14	
Incorrect Answer	*Number*		*Incorrect Answer*	*Number*	
1/4	1		1/4	1	
1/2	16		1/2	2	
1	2		3	3	
1/1	2		4 1/3	1	
1 1/2	2		5	3	
Ends	2		10	1	
No answer	1		25	1	
			28	1	
			30	1	
			t	1	

---

[1] These are actual test results randomly selected from four fifth grade classes of disadvantaged children.

Third Problem

Correct Answer	Number of Children
99	2

Incorrect Answer	Number
1/4	1
7	1
10	4
11	2
17	1
21	1
34	1
37	2
39	4
42 1/2	1
50	1
60	3
66	3
71	1
30/2	1

I have by now identified all the children who will be in each arithmetic group. The advanced group will have five children. This group may have a chance to learn the scope and sequence for the fifth grade: equivalent fractions, higher and lower terms, improper fractions, addition of fractions with unlike denominators. They will not all learn it, but at least they will learn some of it. The other 25 will be in groups ranging from second to fourth grade level. They will repeat once more what they have gone through once, twice, or three times before. I, of course, hope they will do better, but if I am objective, I cannot be optimistic.

The story that is told above poses the problem that will be examined in this book. Many readers may relegate it to science fiction, but teachers of the disadvantaged will recognize it as an everyday occurrence, and all too real. How did these children spend four years in school, an hour a day on arithmetic, taught by competent teachers trained in modern techniques, and learn so little of the meaning and usage of mathematics? What happens that these lessons which sound so reasonable and look so logical and have been so carefully worked out by experienced professional educators, just do not work with so many children?

An analysis and continuation of this story will be found in Chapter 5. Chapters 1 through 4 present a condensed outline of the authors' approach to this dilemma. The reader may wish to obtain an overview at this time, in which case we would suggest reading these chapters in sequence. However, if the reader wishes, he may turn directly to Chapter 5, using Chapters 1 to 4 for reference as needed.

1

Overview of
Natural Mathematics

THE BASIC FLAW IN TRADITIONAL APPROACHES,
"OLD" OR "NEW"

The authors believe that the teaching procedures which will
be presented here are consistent consequences of what is known
about children, especially the disadvantaged child. If they
seem to be radical departures from current practices, the authors believe it to be the current practices which do not conform to all that is known. We suggest that current programs
have failed the disadvantaged child because they persistently
have emphasized one basic teaching convention, in spite of
sporadic modifications. *That underlying convention is that skills
and concepts [1] must be learned before they are applied to a
problem, and that, therefore, they must be taught separately
from their application.* A perceptive examination of even the
most modern textbooks will reveal that this convention is opera-
tive, although it may be unrecognized.

---

[1] The term "skills" is used throughout the book to refer to computational
skills; the term "concepts" is used to refer to generalizations concerning the
nature of mathematical structure.

The authors emphatically reject this convention. If we are to meet the needs of the young child, and if we are to lead him into the world of analytic language and formal mathematics, we must begin with his own intuitive learning processes, in which skills and concepts are not isolated from problem-solving, but, in fact, develop in the process of problem-solving experiences.

The authors believe that the approaches which this book presents do conform to the perceptual-cognitive-motivational components of the young child's learning process. They believe that the procedures are internally consistent and offer the teacher a sequential program. They suggest that adoption of this program will do much to counteract the alienation of the disadvantaged child, and many advantaged children, from school and formal learning. They believe it will add helpful insights for every educator concerned with the young child as a learner in any area. That is to say, the principles and techniques of this approach are not confined to mathematics education. The authors consider them equally pertinent to other areas, although mathematics is perhaps the field in which unsatisfactory techniques have the most obvious consequences. Thus, although elementary teachers will find the discussions framed in mathematical context, they also will find them reflective of general problems and suggestive of solutions in the general curriculum. Secondary teachers engaged in remedial difficulties will find them relevant both to the causes of these difficulties, and to the kind of techniques needed to ameliorate them. Student teachers and educators dealing with teacher preparation will find them a stimulant to critical analysis of the relationship between educational psychology and the real teaching world of the classroom.

With this book, the authors present a model and a program for introducing the young child into the action of what may be termed *Natural Mathematics.* Although we believe that the procedures discussed herein are advantageous in the teaching of all children, we believe that for the disadvantaged they are essential.

We do not maintain that these procedures must be used exclusively. We do maintain that the persistent failure with the disadvantaged is attributable to their insufficient use. We are predicating our presentation on the assumption that disadvantaged children may achieve far beyond their present level with appropriate procedures which engage their potential. We also are presuming that the reader is familiar with the diagnoses of the disadvantaged, in reference to specific deficits in motivation, "lesson" attention span, self-discipline, reward deferment, language development, self-concept, etc.

TEN MAJOR PRINCIPLES OF NATURAL MATHEMATICS FREQUENTLY VIOLATED BY CURRENT PROCEDURES

1. *Skills are not separated and learned first and applied later to a problem.* They are learned in the process of solving many problems.
2. *Neither are concepts separated and learned first and then applied later to a problem.* They are also learned in the process of solving many problems. This is in opposition to the current procedure of using many exercises to illustrate a concept.
3. *Natural Mathematics is, in fact, social action or social experience, which takes place in the process of distribution.*
4. *The unity of problem-solving, skills and concepts demands the integration of subject matter areas.*
5. *The initial problems presented to the child are "real" problems, in that his actual environment is altered by his process of solution.* Hypothetical problems (word problems) are not "real," in this sense, and are used only when they are modified reconstructions of prior real experiences. The child progresses through a theoretical *Role-Playing Hierarchy,* as a wider range of hypothetical problems become psychologically real.
6. The child progresses through a theoretical, problem-solving *Media-Action Hierarchy.* That is, children can solve problems at different media and action levels—first *real,* then *representational,* and finally *symbolic.* At the real media and action level, neither representations nor symbols are necessary, nor should they be involved until the child is able to solve problems without them. Failure in motivation

and comprehension is often attributable to premature use of the symbolic prior to internalization of the action. The representational steps within the real-representational-symbolic model provide the child with the bridge between Piaget's "concrete operational" and "abstract operational" stages, by allowing the child to use concrete operations with semi-abstract materials.

7. *The unity of problem-solving, skills and concepts permits use of both convergent and divergent thinking.* It assures a balance between the two, in which the divergent is given full possibility. At least it is assured that it will not be inhibited.

8. *The unity of problem-solving, skills and concepts also permits the use of either extrinsic or intrinsic rewards.* However, the procedure leads to greater use of intrinsic rewards, since the rewards make up the substantive content of the problems. That is, the experiences more often will be rewarding than rewarded.

9. *The unity of problem-solving, skills and concepts in the introductory phase of mathematics will provide a safe foundation for their eventual separation, for the purpose of refinement at more complex levels of computation and manipulation.* Adherence to the progression of the Media-Action Hierarchy will allow the child to keep the developing skills integrated.

10. *The unity of problem-solving, skills and concepts reduces to a minimum the problem of transfer.* When skills and concepts are taught first, separate from application, transfer is added to the problem of learning. The techniques of Natural Mathematics, on the other hand, do not teach skills in isolation, by which problems may later be solved provided the child is able to transfer. Natural Mathematics engages the child in problems wherein the skill used is precisely what he does in the "solving action."

TRANSFER, INTUITION AND MOTIVATION

The current teaching procedures of mathematics (including "new math"), in which skills and concepts are taught separately from problems, and then later applied, require three transfer learnings by the child. (1) In order to teach a skill or concept, specific, discrete, tangible, and later representational illustrations may be used, but the child is asked to disregard their individuality in favor of the generalized skill or concept which is illustrated by them. (2) When it is felt that the child has acquired this skill or concept as a general principle or policy, the child is then asked to apply it to a specific problem. (3) When the child has solved the problem, whether correctly or incorrectly, he is required to identify and justify the generalized skill and concept he employed.

The purpose of this third transfer-action is to ascertain that the problem was solved by a conscious choice of skill or concept. The teacher wants to be quite sure that the child did not use only intuition to solve the problem. The possibility that the child solved the problem through intuition only is viewed as unsatisfactory and accidental. It is felt that intuition is untrustworthy; it may have produced a correct result in this instance, but is likely to produce incorrect results in others.

It is an illusion, however, that conscious choice of a skill or concept bypasses intuition, or replaces it. Intuitive ability is the essential source for learning at all stages, including the conscious choice of skill or concept itself. Intuition is the initial platform for the beginning learner, the vehicle for progress of the intermediate learner, and the means of breakthrough to new knowledge by the advanced scholar. At all steps along the way, intuition is used as the ultimate appeal when systematized comprehension breaks down, whether its purpose is "remedial" or creative. The authors maintain that premature separation of skills and number concepts from the action of problem-solving suppresses and abuses intuition.

The persistent practice of separation of skills and concepts from their application in problem-solving also reflects the fact that skills and concepts are the primary focus of current teaching procedures. Acknowledging that the interest of the child facilitates learning, current teaching procedures attempt to relate skills and concepts to the child's interests whenever possible. However, in the event of a conflict between the skill-and-concept goals and the child's interests, it is the interests and not the goals which are sacrificed.

The choice of educator-goals over child-interest drastically reduces the intensity of the child's motivation, especially the disadvantaged child's. The middle-class child has had the opportunity to learn, over a considerable pre-school period, to adapt external goals to himself. He has learned that demonstration of his mastery of skills and concepts is evidence of achievement and he is ready to strive for it for its own sake. If he can be interested in the content, so much the better. The disadvantaged child, on the other hand, is much less likely to have developed this attitude. He is generally unable to accept the educator's goals as his own, even though he may be willing to accept the educator's authority.

The integrated techniques of Natural Mathematics retain the motivation which the child's interest engenders, by permitting the child to develop the skills and concepts himself in the process of, and as the process of, satisfying his own interests.

THE REASON FOR THE PRESENT DILEMMA

It is the authors' view that the emergency now facing educators of the disadvantaged is not caused so much by the disadvantaged being a *different type* of child, or having different learning processes (frequently called "learning styles"), or different motivational systems. Rather, it is caused mainly by the disadvantaged child's inadequate preparation for school during his early developmental years at home. This inadequate preparation now confronts educators with the unavoidable problem of dealing with early childhood conceptual and motivational development. The characteristics generally ascribed to the disadvantaged are those found in the much younger non-disadvantaged child. Had general educational practices been proficient in nurturing the child's construction of reality, the disadvantaged child would not appear now as a foreigner to the educational scene, but primarily as a pupil on an earlier developmental level. Our present crisis, focusing on our failure with the disadvantaged, is thus symptomatic of the inadequacy of traditional primary programs.

Natural learning is as natural for the disadvantaged child as for the middle-class child. The disadvantaged child's "cultural difference" is emphasized primarily because traditional school instruction is unnatural. When we speak of learning styles as applied to traditional school programs, we in fact are speaking of adaptations to unnatural learning experiences.

In mathematics, in particular, teaching programs have presupposed an already existing logico-mathematical base on the part of the child, as well as an achievement-motivation syndrome. In other words, it has been assumed that we could appeal to the child's logical reasoning, and that his presence in school implied a learning-orientation of his attention. The program of Natural Mathematics assumes neither of these conditions, and is offered as a theoretical and procedural program for their development.

In summary, Natural Mathematics respects and utilizes the child's natural learning processes, in which skills and concepts grow out of the child's actions of problem-solving, as he becomes confident and is able consciously to view and reflect upon his choices and actions, and subsequently categorize them into unifying images of his own behavior, the internal consistency of which constitutes his structure of mathematics.

2

The Media-Action Hierarchy

How the Child Moves from the Real
to the Symbolic: A Sequential Development
of the Modes of Problem-Solving

In Natural Mathematics children learn mathematical actions by using one-to-one correspondence in real or role-playing experiences, to solve or to resolve problems of distribution in the real world. They experience distributions and the distributing operations of dividing, adding, multiplying, subtracting, by matching. The essential method of distribution is matching. The technique of matching is not separate from the trial and error, problem-solving, discovery method. There is no break between "understanding of a problem" and "the computation of the right answer." The process of matching encompasses both.

FROM DISTRIBUTING (MATCHING) REAL OBJECTS TO COMPUTING WITH SYMBOLS

The transition from matching to computation by using symbols is a major developmental jump. Symbolic computation is a device used to shorten the time it takes to solve a problem. It cannot be used until the action of the problem is solved, or at least until a decision to make a certain "trial" is reached. It may shorten the time it takes to make each trial, but it has no central place or role in the problem-solving strategy. Computational proficiency may be obtained through the use of computational drills. Such drills are often called "problems," but are of quite a secondary order and may be more clearly understood if they are termed "exercises." The child is the "computer" in these exercises.

The main challenge in teaching mathematics is to help the child use the "computer," in solving problems, to help him know what to put into it, and how and when. In order to do this, he must know what computational processes to use, and he must know these before the computer can become useful to him. He will learn these in live matching situations, in which the action of distribution by the child *is* the computation.

Distribution by matching seems time consuming only after the child has become proficient in distributing action, and computation activity begins to separate itself in the mind of the child. At that time, he is ready to shorten the time it takes to solve the problem and he is ready for the short-cut. Symbolic computation, a short-cut, implies all the real life action and operations. They are still there. Just as the word "dog" implies a real dog, the number "7" implies a distribution or redistribution operation (experience). Although the young child may be taught the symbol for "dog" by a simple conditioning process in which the word "dog" is presented contiguously with the real perceptual experience of the dog, the same process cannot be successfully used when symbols represent complex distribution actions. We are not requiring the child to respond merely to the name of a thing, but we are asking him to re-live a complex experience of things and actions.

It is maintained by the authors that in moving from the original perceptual experience of an event, to the mathematical symbol of it, children are forced to take more complex leaps than in any other area of learning. The authors believe this to be the main reason for the special difficulty which many children, and especially the culturally disadvantaged, have with learning mathematics.

A STEP-BY-STEP PROGRESSION FROM THE CONCRETE TO THE ABSTRACT

There are many ways the child can participate in the problem-solving process, however, before he reaches the symbolic level. Each of them will move him along a concrete to symbolic hierarchy, in graduated steps. By the time he reaches the symbolic jump, it will be a much smaller leap than it is customarily. It will also be a more natural transition since the symbolic will not be presented as an alien entity which needs to be interpreted back to reality. It will be just another step in a series of short-cuts.

The most time consuming activity is to deal with the real, with tangible objects in the real world. They are sometimes heavy and difficult to move around; they are sometimes difficult to procure, etc. Sometimes a decision to redistribute is irreversible (for instance, cutting apples). Therefore, it is necessary to use substitutes for the real, and in mathematics we often take it for granted that such substitutes are automatically meaningful. But even the first step in moving away from the "real" is a large jump for a child. It is therefore suggested that children should not be required to use representational material to solve distribution problems until they are quite familiar and at home with the concrete materials, and until they are quite able to solve similar problems using real things and people.

THE INTERMEDIATE REPRESENTATIONS OF THE OBJECTS AND OF THE ACTIONS

Children then may be guided to substitute representational things for the real things. Models or cut-outs of the real items may be distributed or redistributed. It is important that the representation still be handled and physically distributed by the child. It is a matter of the child "pretending" that the representations are the real things. It is necessary for the child to understand that he may behave toward representations of real objects in the same way as he behaved toward the real objects. The important thing is that he is required to learn only one thing at a time. He is required to do with the representations only what he has already done with the real objects. He still physically moves the representations as he did the real objects. In this sense the use of models and cut-outs may not constitute much of a time saver, although it does help him on his journey from the concrete to the abstract.

The next step toward saving time may be the use of physical things which may be moved and distributed physically by the child but which do not now retain any perceptual identification with the real objects or the models except that they are tangible and movable. These may be counting sticks or any other arbitrary small matching devices. They may still be used in dramatic situations, and the one-to-one correspondence method of solving and resolving distribution problems is still maintained. Once again, the child is asked to learn only one thing—he is asked to behave toward the neutral matching items as he behaved toward the cut-outs or the models. The neutral items now represent the real objects. He still solves his problems in the same manner, by physically moving the items about.

The next phase is a major jump for the child. He leaves the three-dimensional world altogether, in order to save time. He moves to the two-dimensional representational world for action as well as objects. In this world he may not physically move objects in order to distribute or redistribute. He must use a representational mode for the action of distribution as well as the objects distributed.

In the first step of this phase, the child draws pictures of the objects and/or people which constitute the elements of the problem. He then learns by trial and error and by the help of the teacher that the one-to-one correspondence, or distributing action, may be represented with circles, lines, and arrows. At this step he again is asked to learn only one thing: that physical action as well as things may be represented two-dimensionally on paper and that he may still control all the elements of the problem. He is still required to be the prime mover of the events. He should be presented with this method only after he is fully capable of solving the problem without it. It should be used as an approach toward time saving.

The next major step will save considerable time. In small gradations the child has learned that many of the visual elements of the drawings of the objects and people are not necessary for efficient representational activity. That is, the drawings of the things and people become more and more abstract. The final stage for objects would be simple marks as are used in the tally system. These abstract marks have been freed from the perception of the child, in that none of the visual characteristics of the original objects or people are retained. The only quality retained at this stage is that each element (object and person) is represented separately. That is, each element is represented by one mark. One apple, one mark, two apples, two marks, etc. The child is required to learn only one thing: that he may behave with the marks as he behaved with the representational drawings. The action representations remain the same, lines, circles, arrows, etc. The marks are matched and distributed as before.

He is now at the last representational phase. He has been freed from the tangible, concrete, "real" world, in that his real world has been internalized, and he may behave toward the marks as he would behave toward the real elements in the problem. He is able to reverse his operations as he would with real elements, by erasing wrong trials, beginning again, and checking on the results. He will now be able to save considerable time and yet feel comfortably at home with his representations. To learn Roman numerals is a small step.

THE USE OF SYMBOLS AND COMPUTATIONS AS SHORT-CUTS FOR SOLUTIONS ALREADY DISCOVERED

The next jump, of course, is into the language of symbols, in which individual elements are not represented individually, in which one-to-one correspondence is no longer possible as a method for solving distribution problems. The child no longer distributes the elements or representations of the elements. Computation separates itself from the distributing act.

The direction or process of distribution—that is, the mathematical operation—must be decided upon (solving the action portion of the problem). Then the appropriate computations are employed. It is here that the child behaves as a computer. It is not at all necessary for him to do this in order to solve his problems. It is expedient, however, because it saves time, and it aids in the development of insights into mathematics, since it allows for *more* experiences, in variety and quantity.

For this reason, the symbolic operations should be reached as soon as possible. But they interfere with learning if they do not grow out of real problem-solving experiences. The experiences must be internalized before the symbolic language becomes meaningful. Otherwise not only is the computation separated from the problem, but so is the child.

In the following Media-Action Hierarchy, there are five teaching principles which apply to each Phase.

1. The sequential development is to be used as an avenue of regression, as well as progression. It maps not only the natural advances of the child, but also the natural retreats to a platform of security. When a child has advanced too far, or too soon, he is to be guided back to the nearest secure platform, until he is ready for another step. In any event, for any tentative advance of any child, the regression to a lower Phase serves him as a way of checking his accuracy and maintaining his centrality.

2. In the first four Phases, the role of mathematical language (numerals, operational signs, relation signs, etc.) is that of language arts. Their purpose is to enable the child to describe, reflect upon, and evaluate what he has already done. They are not to be introduced as problems themselves, nor as the means of solving problems, but rather as a way of communicating about the child's resolution which has already taken place. It is not until the child has progressed through the developmental sequential program, that the symbols themselves are used as means for solving problems.

3. Within each Phase of the Media-Action Hierarchy, the

child's role in problem-solving will be in transition. Initially, his problems will involve concrete outcomes to himself; he will get or keep the results of his solution. When the child is able to solve these problems equitably and efficiently, he will begin to solve various levels of hypothetical problems. (See Chapter 3 for discussion of the sequential development of the child's role in problem-solving.)

4. Although the Media-Action Hierarchy is presented in discrete stages, the child will most often be at several stages simultaneously, in dealing with different kinds of problems of varying difficulty and complexity. As simple problem-solving processes are assimilated at the concrete level (Phase I), similar problems may be moved into the representational sequence (Phases II, III, IV). Meanwhile, problem-solving at the concrete level continues for problem-situations of greater complexity.

5. The Media-Action level of the child's solutions is not identifiable as a function of chronological age. As Piaget's developmental stages were reached at different ages by different children, the children working in any Phase of Natural Mathematics' hierarchies will also vary widely by age. However, in general, we might expect to find a large number of 4–7 year old children in Phases I and II, a large number of 7–9 year old children in Phases III and IV, and a large number of children 10–11 years old and over working in Phase V. On the other hand, a gifted child may already have progressed through the Media-Action and Role-Playing Hierarchies by the age of 6. In this case, it is not suggested that he be required to recapitulate his development simply because he has started school. However, a 15 year old student who is a persistent failure in mathematics may well need to be regressed on the Media-Action and Role-Playing Hierarchies all the way back to Phase I.

In any event, each child will be solving different types of problems on different levels, according to the complexity of the problem and according to the child's previous experiences with the elements and the action involved.

For the purpose of a broad view, we suggest that the above principles be kept in mind as applying at any level of the following program of sequential development.

AN OUTLINE OF THE MEDIA-ACTION HIERARCHY

Phase I.   Media: Real objects
               Actions: Matching, counting

Phase II.   Media: Tangible representations of real objects
                         (movable, exchangeable)
               Actions: Matching, counting

Phase III.   Media: Two-dimensional representations of real
                         objects (picture-drawing)
               Actions: Representational matching (lines, ar-
                         rows, etc.), counting

Phase IV.   Media: Abstract representations (tally marks)
               Actions: Representational matching (lines, ar-
                         rows, etc.), counting, as in Phase III

Phase V.   Media: Numerals
               Actions: Computations

Phase VI.   Media: Algebraic symbols
               Actions: Algebraic operations

The outline that follows condenses the procedure of each Phase.

PHASES I TO VI
SAMPLE PROBLEM-SOLUTION IN EACH PHASE

Phase I

MEDIA: *Real objects*
     Money, candy, gum, toys, etc.
ACTIONS: *Matching, counting*
     A. *Multiple unit matching ("wholes")*
          Social problems which are solved by exchange of whole units.
          Sample problem: Each child is provided with 9 mints and 3 pennies. He is to make exchanges with other

children, as he can, to achieve whatever redistribution he desires.

Solution at this level: Matching and exchange.

B. *Partitioned unit matching ("fractions")*

Social problems which are solved by dividing units before distribution.

Sample problem: Four children are provided with one package of clay. The children are to divide the clay evenly.

Solution at this level: Trial and error marking, cutting and evening-out (corrections).

Phase II

MEDIA: *Tangible representations of real objects (movable, exchangeable substitutes for the real)*

Cut-outs, models, sticks, bottle caps, buttons, washers, cardboard, cloth, string, etc.

ACTIONS: *Matching, counting*

A. *Multiple unit matching ("wholes")*

Sample problem: Same as Phase I problem.

Solution at this level: Bottle caps and play pennies are used instead of mints and real pennies, for the trading. They may later be exchanged for the real.

B. *Partitioned unit matching ("fractions")*

Sample problem: Same as Phase I problem.

Solution at this level: The division is to be made by cutting paper the size of the clay, and repeating until the paper division is as even as possible. Each child makes a paper pattern, and may use it to make his cut of the clay.

Phase III

MEDIA: *Two-dimensional representations of real objects (picture-drawing)*

The child is now guided into drawing on paper all of the elements of the problem, including objects and/or people.

ACTIONS: *Representational matching (lines, arrows, circles, etc.),*
    counting
    The child is also guided into drawing the matching-action.

Phase III is particularly important, since it is the initial pencil-and-paper level. It frees the child and teacher from the time and difficulties of acquiring and handling tangible representations. It provides the possibility of solving problems of greater complexity. It allows problems to be solved in advance. It provides a record of the trials, for review, comparison, and reference. It is especially useful in remedial work for the older child, as a regression level from the symbolic. In developmental work, it demands a structured approach to the problem. At this stage the child is still "constructing" the problem's solution, rather than "computing" it.

    A. *Multiple unit matching ("wholes")*
        Sample problem: John, Mary, Diane, Joe, Bill, Tom, Beth, and Helen are pretending that they are going on a picnic. Each child will want two sandwiches. How many loaves of bread will they have to buy? How much money will they have to spend for the bread? How many slices will be left over?
        Available material: A loaf of bread (for instance, 18 slices), marked with the price (for instance, 22¢).
        Solution at this level:
        STEP 1. Pupil draws all the elements of the problem:
            The children
            The bread each one needs for two sandwiches
            The loaf of bread (after counting the slices)
            The money the loaf costs

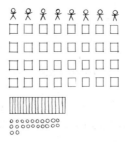

The pupil's solution develops as he adds data and matching actions to *this single drawing*. In order to portray his sequence, the drawing is repeated here for each successive step.

STEP 2. Pupil matches the slices to the bread needed by each child, and discovers that one loaf is not enough.

STEP 3. Pupil draws another loaf, and its cost.

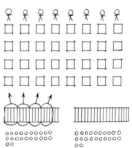

STEP 4. Pupil matches the slices to the bread needed by the remaining children.

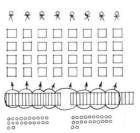

PUPIL COUNTS LOAVES NEEDED: 2
PUPIL COUNTS CENTS NEEDED: 44
PUPIL COUNTS SLICES LEFT OVER: 4

B. *Partitioned unit matching ("fractions")*
Sample problem: Joe, John, Bill, Tom are going to di-

vide a pack of gum. How can they divide it evenly?
Solution at this level:
STEP 1. Pupil draws the elements of the problem.
    The boys
    The gum

STEP 2. Pupil matches "once around."

STEP 3. Pupil draws division of remaining piece, and
    matches parts.

STEP 4. Pupil draws a summary picture of what each
    boy has.

The quantitative problem is now solved, and now the
numerical symbol for the division, 1 1/4, may be introduced as language arts.

Phase IV

MEDIA: *Abstract representations (tally marks)*
    The drawings of the elements of the problem are no longer
    perceptual representations, since the tally marks do not
    resemble the objects for which they stand. The only rep-
    resentational feature of tally marks is that each separate
    object is represented by a separate mark. Tallying is the
    most abstract representation, and is the last step prior to
    the symbolic.

Actions: *Representational matching (lines, arrows, circles, etc.),
    counting, as in Phase III*
   A. *Multiple unit matching ("wholes")*
       Sample problem: Same as Phase III problem.
       Solution at this level: Same solutions as in Phase III,
       using X's for children, and tally marks for the bread
       needed, as well as the slices in the loaf, and the money.
       One of the completed drawing-solutions would be:

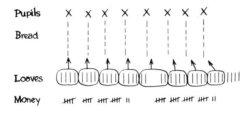

   B. *Partitioned unit matching ("fractions")*
       When tally marks are used to represent parts, in such
       a way as to preserve size relations, they automatically
       revert to being perceptual representations. Therefore,
       in partitioned unit matching, the child will move di-
       rectly from Phase III to Phase V.

Phase V

Media: *Numerals*
Actions: *Computation*
    A numeral symbolizes the objects; an operation symbolizes
    the matching-action.
   A. *Multiple unit matching ("wholes")*
       Sample problem: Same as Phase III problem.
       Solution at this level:
       $8 \times 4 = 32$ (slices needed)
       $32 \div 18 = 1$, remainder 14 (2 loaves needed)
       $2 \times 22\cent = 44\cent$ (money needed)
       $2 \times 18 = 36$ (number slices in the 2 loaves)
       $36 - 32 = 4$ (slices left over)
   B. *Partitioned unit matching ("fractions")*

Sample problem: Same as Phase III problem.
Solution at this level:
5/4 = 1 1/4

Phase VI

MEDIA: *Algebraic symbols*
ACTIONS: *Algebraic operations*

3

The Role-Playing Hierarchy

SEQUENTIAL DEVELOPMENT OF THE CHILD'S ROLE IN PROBLEM-SOLVING

The sequential development of the Media-Action Hierarchy, presented in Chapter 2, offers a progression for the child from the concrete to the abstract, in terms of the materials and methods he uses to solve problems. In Phase I of this progression, the child uses real materials, and his actions are real distributions. He advances through various representational levels until Phase V, when his materials become symbolic numerals and his actions become symbolic computations (and then to Phase VI, where algebraic symbols and operations are used). Thus, the Media-Action Hierarchy refers to the development of the child's "mode" of solving problems.

HOW CHILDREN LEARN TO IDENTIFY WITH PROBLEMS—FROM THE HEDONISTIC AND EGOCENTRIC TO THE IMPERSONAL AND OBJECTIVE

Independent of media and action, there is another theoretical developmental sequence along which the child must advance, if his improved mode of solving problems is to enable him to engage in a wider range of problems. This sequence concerns the child's role in the problems. It begins with the child as hedonistic and egocentric director of his own activities, and ends with the child role-playing as objective director of impersonal activities. Initially, the child's motive is to acquire a concrete outcome, for instance, "how to get candy or money." Eventually, at the highest level of the Role-Playing Hierarchy, he will be able to solve problems which do not relate to him directly, such as problems on the per capita food consumption in various countries.

There are many gradations and variations in the Role-Playing Hierarchy, since the hierarchy refers to the relationship between the child and the problem. Its broad ranges are outlined below:

AN OUTLINE OF THE ROLE-PLAYING HIERARCHY

Phase I.   Real problems and real solutions (outcomes) to the child.

Phase II.   Hypothetical follow-up problems.

Phase III. Hypothetical problems closely related to the child's daily life.

Phase IV.   Hypothetical problems of adults whom the child knows.

Phase V.   General economic, social, and scientific problems.

The following comments may be helpful to the teacher, in moving the child along this progression:

Phase I. Real problems: direct outcome to the child

In this phase, the child's interests are hedonistic and egocentric. He is able to bring his mental energies to problems which involve concrete outcomes to himself. These outcomes are usually tangible, but need not always be. As well as the acquisition of things, they may determine the time he may go for a drink, or the day he is first in the lunch line, or where he sits in the class. Furthermore, these outcomes may evolve from any one of the various modes of problem-solving. For instance, he may acquire candy by trading (Phase I of the Media-Action Hierarchy), or he may compute a mail-order symbolically (Phase V of the Media-Action Hierarchy). In addition, his acquisition may be immediate, as in the former example, or deferred as in the latter. Furthermore, the problem may be either simple or difficult in terms of mathematical complexity. (The progression of complexity of problems will be discussed in the next chapter.)

The primary characteristic of this phase of the Role-Playing Hierarchy is that the child gets or keeps the results of his solution. In fact, he does not play a role at this initial stage, at all; he is just himself. Also, the problem itself is real, not hypothetical. The child is not asked to imagine that he has such a problem; he has it.

Phase II.   Hypothetical follow-up variations of real problems

These are hypothetical variations of real problems which the child has already solved:

Suppose that the child has just traded two pennies (out of three which he had) for four mints. The teacher asks what the child might have done if he had been given four pennies; or what he might have done if the mints had been lollipops. The child's solution is an imagined variation of his previous real actions. The child is not asked to play another person's role nor to imagine a new pattern of action. However, the circumstances become hypothetical; his decisions will not have practical effect.

Phase III.   Hypothetical original problems closely related to the child's daily life

Although these problems differ from the real problems already solved, they have a close relevance to the child's life-situation:

Suppose that the child received a dollar for his birthday. How will he spend it? Suppose that he and four other boys buy a bag of thirty marbles. How many will each get? The child remains central because the problems refer to his own past experiences and his immediate possibilities.

Hypothetical problems of this type may be phrased in terms of another person's circumstances and actions:

Suppose Mary receives a dollar for her birthday. How will she spend it? Suppose five boys buy a bag of marbles, etc. This type of problem remains in the Phase III category although it is worded in terms of a person other than the child, since the other person's needs and activities are similar to the child's. These are problems which he recognizes he *could* have, and can imagine himself having, and therefore can accept as if they were his own.

Phase IV. *Hypothetical problems of adults (people he knows)*

These are hypothetical problems which do not necessarily relate to the child's immediate situation, but which involve the situation of others whose lives and problems are different. At the beginning of this phase, the problems should at least concern others whom the child knows well, who are engaged in activities which affect the child's surroundings:

Suppose that Mother is buying material to make curtains for six windows, etc. Later in this phase, the problems may concern others more removed from the child, and who are engaging in activities which have no immediate bearing on his own situation: Suppose that a boy has a part-time job, and is saving half of what he makes to buy a motorcycle. The motorcycle he wants costs $175. He makes $15 a week. How long does he have to save until he can buy the motorcycle?

The child is able to bring his attention to these problems when he is able to play the role of others. These are genuine roles and require that the child pretend that he is indeed someone else; however, he still can see a realistic possibility that these problems might become his own, in the foreseeable future. These Phase IV problems cannot be changed into Phase III problems by rewording in the "second person," that is, by re-stating as, "Suppose *you* have a part-time job and are saving. . . ." In fact, it is just this which makes them essentially different from Phase III problems—their content is not relevant to the child's present problems. The distinction between Phase III and Phase IV is thus a substantive difference and not merely a grammatical variation. For instance, the problem, "Suppose Mary went to the store with a quarter, and. . . .", if judged by the language structure, might seem like a Phase IV problem. Superficially, it would seem to be a problem requiring the child to suppose that he or she were Mary. In fact, it *is* a Phase III problem for any child accustomed to going to the store, because Mary could very well be he. That is, her problem could very well be his.

A teacher will often recognize that a real Phase IV problem is beyond a child's role-playing ability. She will paraphrase the problem in an attempt to bring it closer to the child by the device, "Now look, let's look at the problem this way. Suppose that *you*. . . ." Sometimes this may be effective. Often, however, the child and problem remain disconnected, in spite of the attempt. They will remain disconnected until the child has learned to identify with a wider range of persons, and their activities and interests. This, however, is not a process of mathematics education, but of social experiences and language arts. On the other hand, if a Phase III problem has a Phase IV type of wording, as in the example, "Suppose Mary went to the store with a quarter. . . .", the teacher will not have to reword it. If the experiences in the problem are like the child's own, he will process the information of the problem into a personal story himself.

This is not to say that the rewording of a problem into a "Suppose *you*" form should be avoided. In the borderline areas, where the child is almost able to play the role, the suggestion may be sufficient. However, it should be recognized that the effort will only be successful in these cases. Therefore, it should not be relied upon as a technique which will solve a real role-playing difficulty. Nor should the teacher feel that the difficulty is a result of her inability, somehow, to rephrase the problem more clearly. The difficulty is caused by the role-playing demands of the problem, which are beyond the child's readiness.

The teacher may recall particular pairs of problems, which involve precisely the same mathematics for solution. She may feel a sense of despair that the children seem able to solve the one but not the other. She may even tell the children that the two problems are just alike. "You solve the second one just like you did the first." But to the child, they are not alike. In one, he is able to identify with the elements; in the other, he is not.

Phase V. General economic, social, and scientific problems

In these problems, the real or possible connection of the child with the characters and events of the problem is removed. Examples of this type of problem would include:

Suppose three men go into business together. One invests $2,000; one invests $4,000; one invests $6,000. The first year they make a profit of $3,000. Problem: How should they divide it? Or the exercise: A mile is 5,280 feet. How many yards is it?

The child is prepared for this level only when he has adopted problem-solving as a satisfying activity for its own sake.

The most difficult transition for the child to make is the move from real problems to hypothetical problems. In this move, his desire to acquire must be replaced by a desire simply to resolve. His new motivation will depend on his ability to accept resolutions themselves as rewarding outcomes. So he must feel dissatisfaction with the unresolved aspects of the problem story. Hypothetical problems are necessary, however, for two reasons: (1) There is a limit to the number and type of arithmetic problems which can be solved by real media and real actions in a real classroom, and (2) if twelve years of education are to equip the child to deal with mathematical problems in his adult life, he must be accelerated beyond his daily-life experiences either in or out of the classroom. The hypothetical word-problem is an indispensable mediator.

It is essential that the transition process, from real to hypothetical, begin where the hypothetical can be tied in very closely with the real. This tie-in is created by the teacher's presentation of problems which are variations of the real problem the child has just solved. We have described these variations in Phase II. The child's ability to respond to these variations again emphasizes the importance of language arts. Language arts builds the hypothetical "mental set."

THE CONTINUING IMPORTANCE OF THE REAL, FOR REGRESSION AND REFERENCE

As the child becomes successful in solving hypothetical problems, it should not be concluded that he no longer needs to experience solving real problems. The solving of real problems should be used as a regression level, and as a renewal of the child's identification with quantitative activities. In this regard, mathematics does not differ from any other area of studies, as, for instance, social studies, where the child's learning about various forms of social organization should be related back to classroom social organization. It should not be forgotten that most of the adult, out-of-school, everyday problems are at the Phase I level, from the adult's viewpoint. However, from the child's viewpoint, these same problems involve role-playing on higher levels of the hierarchy.

Thus, if the child succeeds in moving from Phase I to Phase II, from the real to the hypothetical, even in the most personal form, and can solve Phase I and Phase II problems rationally, accurately, and efficiently, the achievement will be substantial. The child will have learned to adopt the role which is sufficient for solution of (or participation in) most of the adult mathematics he will need. This, of course, is particularly true for the disadvantaged child. But it opens for him, at the same time, the mental set for further advancement to the limit of his intellectual capacity.

4

Complexity of
Problem Hierarchy

The final hierarchy concerns the complexity of problems. This hierarchy resembles the traditional scope-and-sequence, in that the solutions of the progressively complex problems will parallel the usual sequence of "skills and concepts." The crucial difference between the hierarchy of Natural Mathematics, as compared with the usual sequence, is the thematic difference in viewpoint as to what is being developed: the child or the mathematics.

EMPHASIS ON THE DEVELOPMENT OF THE CHILD'S RATIONAL STRUCTURE RATHER THAN DEVELOPMENT OF MATHEMATICAL STRUCTURE

The traditional scope-and-sequence (including "new math") is a development of mathematics. This approach concentrates on the logical and rational development of mathematical skills and concepts. The system is internally consistent. But it does not necessarily develop quantitative, rational, logical thinking in the hedonistic, egocentric child. It rather assumes that the child is already capable of this type of thinking. The identifying characteristic of this approach is the primary use of lesson presentation, followed by exercises. The new skill or concept is presented, explained, illustrated or "discovered" by a set of examples. They are usually exercises themselves, differing only in that the teacher or the text shows the child how to do them. They are usually followed by a number of drill-exercises which the child does himself, if he can. Only lastly are "word problems" presented, which require application of the skills and concepts just "learned," and, incidentally, demonstrate to the pupil that such application exists.

The hierarchies of Natural Mathematics, on the other hand, relate to the conceptual and motivational development of the child. The Complexity Hierarchy is a progression of problems which may be either real or hypothetical. They involve increasingly complex processes of solution.

EXERCISES VERSUS PROBLEMS

It is, therefore, important to examine the difference between an exercise and a problem, from the child's point of view.

A mathematics exercise has the same characteristic as a physical exercise. It is a repeated use of skills—calisthenics—so that they develop, are retained, and are kept toned up. A singer practices the scale for tone precision; an athlete jogs to keep in shape; a pupil does mathematics exercises to maintain and increase his skill. An exercise is an isolated set of behavior which relates to nothing beyond itself. It is, therefore, far from a child's direction of intention in terms of egocentric, hedonistic goals. The child must have had many problem-solving experiences before he will appreciate exercises for their intrinsic and future value.[1]

---

[1] He could, however, learn to enjoy exercises because they become comforting, perseverative experiences in which he has succeeded and which he has been rewarded for doing. This is dangerous and leads to splintered learning. Every mathematics teacher is familiar with this splintering. She needs only to think of the moans of distress from her pupils, even some of the best, when her study plans call for "word problems." One of the authors has noted that the tendency to perseverate in exercises persist even among adults returning to school for remedial study. Many of these students who are 25 years of age would still rather do sheet after sheet of computation exercises, than take up a set of problems.

It is sometimes assumed that an exercise may be converted into a problem by posing it in a word-context, that is, by turning it into a "word problem." However, an out-of-context computation, when placed in context, may remain merely a sequential step in a mathematical structure. For instance, "If three boys had eight cents each, how much would they have altogether?" This is simply the 3×8 step between the 2×8 and 4×8 steps of the multiplication table. It is not a problem; it is language arts. "How many do they have altogether," is simply the English language equivalent for "$\times$" or "$+$." There is no reason for knowing the answer. No one has a problem. It is an attempt through language to make a direct transfer application of "3×8" to real problems, but the transfer is really to language.

Since exercises have to do with skills, they are themselves mathematical "language arts" practice. Their main purpose is speed and accuracy, not insight and integration. They are useful as mathematical language arts experiences, but to add the non-mathematical language does not change their basic nature.

An exercise may be turned into a problem when the basic element of a problem is added—that is, motive. There can be no problem without someone *having* a problem. Otherwise it is still a calculation exercise or drill. The exercise cited above could be developed into a problem, for instance, if the total amount of money was crucial information for making a decision about what could be done with the money. But the problem would not *ask* how much they had altogether. The decision to find this out would be an integral part of the problem's solution—its first step. That is, a problem is not just a question; it is a situation out of which something really must happen.

For the young child, a problem must, in fact, be a dramatic situation—real or play—to be acted out, with all its elements coordinated spatially, temporally, and socially. It should demand an integration of the child's entire repertory of strategies and understandings. (And, in order to be so used, they must have been developed in an integrated fashion.) He must discriminate between the elements which are different from categories of previous problems and those which are similar. In short, he must analyze and make choices. In order to mobilize the child's participation, the dramatic unresolved situation must either have direct personal consequences to him or he must be able to identify to some degree with the problem.

FIVE PREREQUISITES OF A PROBLEM

In summary, the ideal characteristics of a problem for the young child are:

1. The skills and concepts should not stand in his way. There must not be too many. They must not dominate the problem.
2. The child should be familiar with the elements of the problem.
3. Someone must get something or exchange something, or use the information to decide to do something.
4. If it is a hypothetical problem, the child must be able to identify with the characters of the story.
5. The characters must not be merely a gimmick to get the child to solve a problem which he does not accept as a real problem. That is, the problem should allow the child to role-play other non-quantitative aspects of the situation as well as the quantitative aspects. A child enjoys being someone else. He naturally is able and eager to play many roles. Going from one to another creates no difficulty in free dramatic role-playing: playing school, house, doctor, cowboys and Indians. These situations the child imitates, imagines and invents. When introducing quantitative elements into a situation, these non-quantitative elements should not be suppressed; the child should remain free to invent dialogue and dramatic possibilities and consequences of the situation. In short, if the dramatic situation is limited to only a restricted quantitative problem and outcome, to this extent the child will be less willing to offer his fullest imaginative capabilities.

Exercises should *follow* real or hypothetical problems, to sharpen skills and to reinforce the processes used in the problems. They may also introduce variations and modifications of the quantitative elements, drawing the child's attention to the relevance of the quantitative aspects to the problem's outcome.

THREE PRINCIPLES OF COMPLEXITY
OF PROBLEM HIERARCHY

Since the Natural Mathematics sequential program is based on problem-solving action, the currently practiced scope and sequence of complexity will be somewhat altered. There are general similarities, in that they both move from small to large whole numbers, simple to complex fractions, one-step to multi-step problems. Dissimilarities include the following:

1. In Natural Mathematics, symbolic operations develop out of tangible and representational operations. Thus, addition, subtraction, multiplication, and division are not formally separated in the early stages.
2. Another difference is the acceleration, in Natural Mathematics, of the development of problem-solving concepts, but without the necessity of their conceptual categorization. Introductory problems involve all four operations, and fractions as well as whole numbers. However, their categorization is an outgrowth of the child's observation of his own problem-solving behavior. That is, the categories are not presented to the child as the real substance of his instruction. They are not defined at the first moment of possible comprehension. They are not formalized at all, until the child is proficient in their appropriate uses.
3. A corollary of this difference is that the child does not deal with complex refinements of any operation, until after he is capable of solving simple problems involving many operations. That is, when he learns to count, he need only learn to count as many objects as are involved in the problems he is solving. When he learns to add, his sums need not exceed the sums in these problems. When he learns to use fractions, the denominators need only be those involved in his real problems. After he can solve problems involving all the operations with small distributions, he will then begin the study of larger distributions.

All of these differences, of course, arise from the fact that the sequential development in Natural Mathematics is based on real problems or hypothetical problems of real possibility and interest. Exercises and drill are similarly oriented, and are not expanded beyond credible variations of the problem content.

With these differences, the broad outline of the Complexity Hierarchy may be found in the progression of any series of elementary mathematics textbooks.

SUMMARY OF PROBLEM-SOLVING HIERARCHIES

Three problem-solving hierarchies have been presented which establish a model for the sequential development of each child-problem relationship:

1. Media-Action (materials and methods, or modes)
2. Role-Playing (locus of problem-solver)
3. Complexity (mathematical difficulty)

A NEW WAY OF IDENTIFYING NOT ONLY WHAT-IS-THE-MATTER, BUT WHAT-TO-DO

Although these hierarchies are somewhat correlated, in that the child proceeds upward on each of them, there is great variability in his progress on each dimension, irregularity in his relative advances, and frequent regression on each. Thus there is no fixed pattern of progression. However, if the hierarchies are used as guidelines for the development of the mathematical potentialities of the child, the authors suggest that the breakdowns and impasses, so often experienced by pupils in mathematics, will be substantially lessened. In current mathematics programs, the Media-Action dimension and Role-Playing dimension are often collapsed into the Complexity dimension, taking for granted the child's development, and placing all the emphasis on the development of mathematics. That is, current programs are generally more concerned with the mathematical content of the problem than with the child's perception of the problem.

This emphasis often leads both child and teacher into frustration. When diagnosis of a child's difficulty is made solely on the dimension of complexity of problem, the diagnosis will reveal the "mathematical where" of the difficulty, but often neither the "why" nor the "what to do." In current teaching programs, there is little remedy available to the teacher except to back down on this one dimension and repeat—often finding the pupil stopped again, and at nearly the same place. If the child's real difficulty lies in inadequate sequential development along the other dimensions, the review-and-try-again process may become a vicious shuttle for both teacher and child, as illustrated in the teacher's story in the Prologue. The authors suggest that moving down on the other two hierarchies will more often locate and bring the child through his difficulty. The three hierarchies together thus constitute a new way of appraising the child's achievement, keeping a record of his progress, and indicating the experiences he needs for integrated development.

A DIAGNOSTIC PROFILE OF A CHILD'S PERFORMANCE PATTERN ON TWO PROBLEMS

As an illustration, let us consider the achievement pattern of a child on a problem of the following complexity: 3 steps, numerals to 50, involving multiplication and division successively (e.g., the sample problem on the cost of the bread, used to illustrate Phase III of the Media-Action Hierarchy). Let us say that if this problem is posed as a real problem, on Phase I of the Role-Playing Hierarchy (the class really is going on a picnic), this child can solve it on Phase III of the Media-Action Hierarchy (picture drawing). But if it is posed as a hypothetical problem, on Phase III of the Role-Playing Hierarchy (he *himself* is not going on a picnic), the child may have to regress to Phase II of the Media-Action Hierarchy (match pieces of paper or cardboard and use play money). And if it is posed as a Phase V hypothetical problem (for instance, in the context of the cost of oil used by machines), the child may not be able to solve it at all.

On the other hand, suppose the problem is much lower on the Complexity Hierarchy, for instance, that it involves only a single step and division by 2. If such a problem is posed as a

PROBLEM-SOLVING HIERARCHIES

MEDIA-ACTION HIERARCHY	ROLE-PLAYING HIERARCHY	COMPLEXITY OF PROBLEM HIERARCHY
Phase VI MEDIA: Algebraic symbols ACTIONS: Algebraic operations	**Phase V** General economic, social, and scientific problems	Modified
Phase V MEDIA: Numerals ACTIONS: Computations	**Phase IV** Hypothetical problems of adults	scope
Phase IV MEDIA: Abstract representations (tally marks) ACTIONS: Representational matching, counting		and sequence of
Phase III MEDIA: Two-dimensional representations (picture drawing) ACTIONS: Representational matching, counting	**Phase III** Hypothetical problems related to the child	current mathematics
Phase II MEDIA: Tangible representations ACTIONS: Matching, counting	**Phase II** Hypothetical follow-up variations of real problems	programs
Phase I MEDIA: Real objects ACTIONS: Matching, counting	**Phase I** Real problems. Real outcome to the child	

SYMBOLIC — CONCRETE

IMPERSONAL-OBJECTIVE — HEDONISTIC-EGOCENTRIC

MULTI-STEP, LARGE QUANTITIES, COMPLEX RATIOS — ONE-STEP, SMALL QUANTITIES, SIMPLE RATIOS

PROBLEM-SOLVING HIERARCHIES [2]

MEDIA-ACTION HIERARCHY	ROLE-PLAYING HIERARCHY	COMPLEXITY OF PROBLEM HIERARCHY

SYMBOLIC

Phase VI
MEDIA: Algebraic symbols
ACTIONS: Algebraic operations

Phase V
MEDIA: Numerals
ACTIONS: Computations

Phase IV
MEDIA: Abstract representations (tally marks)
ACTIONS: Representational matching, counting

Phase III
MEDIA: Two-dimensional representations (picture drawing)
ACTIONS: Representational matching, counting

CONCRETE

Phase II
MEDIA: Tangible representations
ACTIONS: Matching, counting

Phase I
MEDIA: Real objects
ACTIONS: Matching, counting

IMPERSONAL-OBJECTIVE

HEDONISTIC-EGOCENTRIC

Phase V
General economic, social, and scientific problems

Phase IV
Hypothetical problems of adults

Phase III
Hypothetical problems related to the child

Phase II
Hypothetical follow-up variations of real problems

Phase I
Real problems. Real outcome to the child

MULTI-STEP, LARGE QUANTITIES, COMPLEX RATIOS

ONE-STEP, SMALL QUANTITIES, SIMPLE RATIOS

Modified

scope

and

sequence

of

current

mathematics

programs

$8 \times 4 = 32$

$32 \div 18 = 1 \text{ R } 14$

$2 \times 22¢ = 44¢$

$10 \div 2 = 5$

---

[2] Lines indicate graphically a child's performance pattern on two problems (as classified by complexity and role).

real problem, this child may be able to solve it on Phase V of the Media-Action Hierarchy (by use of numerical computation). ("John and Joe, you are going to divide 10 pennies. How many should each of you take?") If it is posed as a hypothetical problem, on Phase III of the Role-Playing Hierarchy ("Two girls have to wash the windows on Saturday. Their house has 10 windows. How many does each girl have to wash?"), this child may regress to Phase IV of the Media-Action Hierarchy (use tally marks). If it is posed as a hypothetical problem on Phase V of the Role-Playing Hierarchy ("If a light flashes 10 times in 2 seconds, how many times should it flash in 1 second?"), again this child may not be able to solve it at all.

The diagram on page 71 indicates this child's highest achievement pattern, on the foregoing two complexity levels. It should be interpreted from *right to left:* The ends of the lines show the Media-Action Phase by which the child can solve the problem, for each role required of him. Notice that there is no performance line, for either complexity level, from Phase V of the Role-Playing Hierarchy. At Phases I and III of the Role-Playing Hierarchy, this child is performing successfully.

The ultimate goal, of course, is that all patterns should terminate in a performance line from Phase V of the Role-Playing Hierarchy to Phase V of the Media-Action Hierarchy, and eventually to Phase VI. Many children will have made this advance, on elementary types of problems, before the last year of elementary school.

5

Analysis of the Teacher's Story

CONTINUATION OF THE PROLOGUE

The reader is referred to the teacher's story in the Prologue. The present chapter offers an analysis of the failures experienced by this teacher.

It will be recalled that the Prologue described a fifth grade class of disadvantaged children. It recounted a teacher's repeated efforts to reach them with the basic skills and concepts of mathematics, and the lack of success of these efforts.

Let's go back and examine in some detail where this process begins in our schools. In describing the fifth grade consequences, we used an imaginary account of a particular classroom and teacher. In describing the first grade beginnings, we will use the same approach. Our wish is to be as specific as possible and to emphasize the impact of the instruction on the pupils. Therefore, as before, we will synthesize some of the approaches and suggestions common to current programs, in the following presentation.

A CASE AGAINST EARLY INTRODUCTION OF SETS

A common introductory suggestion is that the child be guided from experiences with concrete aids as sets of things to the concept of number (cardinal number of a set). The initial goal is that the pupil learn the meaning of the term "set," and become familiar with the use of the term. The teacher is usually instructed to develop the meaning of set by using sets that are familiar to the pupils: a set of books, glasses, checkers, a baseball team, etc. She does so, possibly showing a set of crayons, holding up a set of jacks, going to the bookcase and touching a set of books. She may explain that a group of tables is a set of tables. She describes "member of set" in terms of members of a ball team. The children are now asked to apply these explanations to a picture. A picture might be a park scene showing some boys and girls playing games. The picture may include a picnic table and benches, a squirrel. Let's say that one boy is feeding the squirrel; several other boys are playing ball. The children are pleased with the picture and look it over to see who is in it and what they are doing.

The teacher now calls on the children to describe the sets they find in the picture. She asks, "Who can tell me a set in this picture?"

Let's suppose there is no immediate response to this question. The teacher considers several possible questions which might give the children some leads. She can ask, "Who can tell what we said about sets?" She rejects this choice. A confused answer will require that the volunteer pupil be corrected in his first response. She can simply go over the explanation herself. She rejects this choice. She has just directed the children's attention to the picture. She can ask, "Who sees something that there's more-than-one-of?" She rejects this choice. It assumes the child's knowledge of "more than," and the question also implies that one object is not a set. This would contradict the important concept which she must teach later, that a set may contain one object as well as any other number.

She decides to ask what is in the picture, "Who can tell me something in this picture?" Suppose a child replies, "A boy feeding a squirrel." The teacher may now say that's fine and ask him if he sees any other boys in the picture. Several children will reply that there are boys playing ball.

Again the teacher has a choice. She can use this response as a base for explaining that all these boys make up a set, regardless of what they are doing. Or she can try to "elicit" this by asking, "Do all these boys make up a set, regardless of what they are doing?" She chooses in favor of pupil participation, and asks. However, she omits the phrase, "regardless of what they are doing." She sees that its objectivity may not be understood and that it may be received as a warning. This would mislead the children into answering, "No." So she asks, "Do all these boys make up a set?" Let's say the question draws several affirmative replies and nods, from the children who are looking at the teacher. From those who are absorbed in the picture, there are few responses. The teacher now questions the child who answered originally. "Joe, do you think all these boys make up a set?"

If we are going to understand a child's learning experience, one of the things we must be able to do is to put ourselves in his place and imagine his mental responses. We must look at these, of course, because it is these which constitute his learning or failure to learn. Let us imagine that this teacher can "read the child's mind," and that this dialogue takes place between her statements and his thoughts.

TEACHER: Do all these boys make up a set?

PUPIL: That boy is feeding a squirrel. I wonder what he's feeding him?

TEACHER: Do you see the boys playing ball?

PUPIL: Yeah, they're playing catch. I see them.

TEACHER: Do all these boys make up a set?

PUPIL: No, ma'am. There's only one boy feeding a squirrel.

TEACHER: But Joe, all the boys do make up a set, regardless of what they are doing, because they are boys. (Even that squirrel makes up a set of squirrels, because it's a squirrel, even if it's only one squirrel.)

PUPIL: But they aren't playing together. They aren't even anywhere near each other. But that girl is standing by the boy. They might look like a set?

TEACHER: No, sets don't always have to be right next to each other. Boys who belong to a school class are still members even when they're not in school.

PUPIL: I think that boy and girl are a set. She's watching him. And maybe those boys playing ball are a set. Anyway, the boys are playing ball.

TEACHER: Well, how about those trees?

PUPIL: I see some big ones. They look like a set.

TEACHER: There's another tree, though.

PUPIL: I see that one too, but that's just a little tree. It doesn't belong with the big ones. It's different.

TEACHER: (remembering that she should emphasize that the objects in a set need not be alike) You're right, Joe. That tree is different. But things in a set don't have to be just alike. When you buy a set of crayons, don't you get a red one, and a blue one, and a black one, and so forth?

PUPIL: They're a set because they come in the same box. You buy them that way.

TEACHER: Look at the flowers. Do they form a set?

PUPIL: No ma'am. Those flowers are just growing wild.

TEACHER: They form a set, just the same. Now, Joe, I want you to think about the set of all boys in the room. Are you a member of this set?

PUPIL: Sometimes I am. They don't all like me.

TEACHER: Tell me this, are you a boy?

PUPIL: Yes.

TEACHER: Are you in this room?

PUPIL: Yes.

TEACHER: Then you are a member of the set of boys in this room. It doesn't matter if they like you or not, as far as being in the set is concerned.

PUPIL: That's all that matters to me.

TEACHER: Joe, I know that's what is important to you. And I promise, we'll talk about that, too. But right now—even if it doesn't seem important to you—try to think about just that you're a boy and they're boys, and that makes you all a set of boys.

PUPIL: OK, but we don't have a club like you said.

TEACHER: Let's look at it another way. Think about the set of girls in the room. Are you a member of this set?

PUPIL: No, they don't have a club either. I wouldn't even join it if they asked me. But I like Judy. She has some chewing gum. I asked her for a piece before school, but she wouldn't give me any. I'm going to ask her again after lunch. I think she'll give me some. I wonder if she has any left.

Another current approach might begin in a similar way, with the teacher using familiar collections to explain the word "set." The picture which the children study, however, may be formalized, and instead of a single scene containing several natural sets, there are already several obvious pairs of sets: girls and bicycles, shoes and socks, etc.

In each pair, the children are to draw lines to match the members one-to-one. Before having the children do this, the teacher may give several demonstrations, to introduce the idea "as many as" and to show how one-to-one matching can determine this. As one demonstration, she may have a child place a number of rulers on the same number of chairs.

Let's imagine a child's mental responses to this program, as we did previously. Our subject will be a child who is going to become one of our fifth grade slow achievers.

TEACHER: Here is a set of rulers, and here is a set of chairs. How can we tell without counting, if there are as many rulers as chairs?

PUPIL: I'd like to sit in one of those chairs. Then everybody could see me and I could wave to them.

TEACHER: Now Joe, try to think about how many chairs there are, not what you could do with them.

PUPIL: Well, there's plenty. Nobody in them.

TEACHER: Now think about this set of rulers. What we want to do is find out if there are as many rulers as there are chairs.

PUPIL: What does she want to find that out for? Why don't you give us the rulers? Are you going to give us those rulers?

TEACHER: No, we're not going to do anything with the rulers or the chairs, at all, except find out if there are as many rulers as chairs. Joe, you come up and put these rulers on these chairs, just one ruler on each chair.

PUPIL: That's a good idea. I hope I do this right.

TEACHER: Were there any rulers left over?

PUPIL: No, but I've got my ruler on my desk. I can go get that one.

TEACHER: No, Joe, I mean these rulers. Were there any chairs left over?

PUPIL: I wish I could sit in that chair by the teacher's desk and pretend I'm teacher.

TEACHER: Joe, were there any chairs left over?

PUPIL: Left over, left over. She wants me to say "No." No.

TEACHER: Then were there as many rulers as chairs?

PUPIL: Yes, no, yes, no.

TEACHER: Yes.

The children then turn to the lesson-picture and connect the objects of one set to the objects of the other. The teacher asks if any are left over from either set. When the children answer that there are not, the teacher says, "Then there are just as many (bicycles) as (girls)?" The children are to answer "Yes." A later lesson will use a similar technique to develop the concept of "more than" and "fewer than." (The sets in the later pictures will not be in one-to-one correspondence.)

Eventually a lesson will reach the idea of number by asking the children to count the number of things in each set. But if the child has not already learned to count, the set concept is usually tabled while he is taught this skill directly. It is usually suggested that the child be given tangible objects for this purpose. The teacher may be urged to maintain the word "set" when she refers to the objects, but her emphasis at this time is on the child's learning of the number sequence.

The mental dialogue continues:

TEACHER: Joe, here are some soda bottletops. Would you count them and see how many there are? Touch each one, as you count it.

PUPIL: One, two, three, six, seven, ten. Are you going to let us play with these? Wonder what I can do with them. I'd like to throw one over to Mike. Wonder if he could catch it. Maybe we could all throw and catch.

TEACHER: Let me take your hand, here. We'll touch each top, and I'll count and you count right after me, One,

two, three, four, five, six. Now that's six tops. You
just counted them. Let's do it again.

After the teacher has grouped her class for mathematics,
she works in this way with all those who have not learned to
count. Each day, to each child, she gives a number of bottletops and asks them to count them. She increases the number
as each child is able to progress. After several days, Joe's idea
about playing throw-and-catch becomes a reality, and the
teacher throws the bottletops into the trash can. She uses other
concrete objects, also, discarding them as the children devise
distracting uses for them: that toothpicks can be stuck between
the teeth, that paper squares can be licked and stuck to the
face, that washers can be twirled on a pencil and sailed off. In
the end the teacher touches or holds up objects herself as the
children count.

These children do learn to count. They learn to write the
numerals. They learn that $4 + 5 = 9$ and that $5 + 4 = 9$. But
they may never learn that $4 + 5 = 5 + 4$ as a concept, or that
$4 \times 5 = 5 \times 4$ as a concept. They may never learn that $4/5 +
5/4 = 41/20 = 2 \ 1/20$ at all. Even if they do learn this as an
isolated mathematical skill, they often do not retain it. And
even if they retain it, they are almost never able to transfer it
to the solution of problems.

ANALYSIS OF THE VIOLATION OF THE CHILD'S
NATURAL CONCERNS

Let's see what these current approaches have in common.
First, they have common goals: teaching sets, teaching matching, teaching number ideas, teaching rudimentary computation.
In other words, they have the goal of helping the child *substitute quantitative experiencing for qualitative experiencing*.
They aim to teach the child that the essential element of things
is their comparability or interchangeability. For instance, consider the exercise in which the child is to match bicycles to
girls. The purpose of the lesson is to guide the child into experiencing the bicycles as a set, rather than each separately as a

unique bicycle he might ride. It asks the child to eliminate his participation with the bicycles, and substitute the concept of sets. It wishes the child to match the bicycles rather than ride them, and to gain satisfaction from doing so. In the exercise on picking the set of boys out of the picture (or out of the classroom), the goal is the same: to lead the child into experiencing the boys as a set, rather than separately as possible personal relationships. We wish him to experience quantitatively, rationally, and objectively what he naturally would experience qualitatively and egocentrically.

Secondly, these approaches teach the set-skills, set-concepts, and number skills-and-concepts *prior* to any genuine application to a life problem. The child is asked to learn to identify sets, match sets, comprehend the concept of sets, and to count before he has a chance to experience their usefulness or relevance. One might say that the exercises themselves could be considered as problems. But they are not at all problems from the child's life-view. The young child is hedonistic and egocentric. His world is not made up of sets, nor is it made up according to any other quantitative model. (The foregoing lessons were based on sets, because this is the approach recommended by most modern programs.) The child's world, and his problems, are made up of qualitative things and the possibilities of owning them, eating them, playing with them, etc.

When we as educators promote the idea of beginning with the child where he is, we must be certain to examine closely just where he is. The young child, especially the disadvantaged child, does not naturally experience his world quantitatively, objectively, rationally. Therefore, any instructional approach whose major appeal is directed toward these mental processes, as if they already existed in the child, is not child-centered because it bypasses essential stages in the child's mental development. These approaches are interested in the logical and rational development of mathematical skills and concepts. They proceed in a logical, step by step sequence from the simple to the complex. The system is internally consistent, but it does not *develop* quantitative, rational, logical thinking in the hedonistic, egocentric child. It rather assumes that the child is already capable of quantitative thinking and proceeds to present the child with skills and concepts.

The exercises are, in fact, demonstration experiences. They demonstrate the educator's solution to a mathematics problem, which is a problem in the educator's life-view. These programs do not contain children's problems. They ask the child to disregard his own interests in favor of the educator's concern, which is to teach him mathematics.

Thirdly, when the current programs introduce word problems, it is after the skills and concepts have been taught. The word problems are given to the pupil, not to generate his learning of skills and concepts, but to test it. The word problems are still not necessarily children's problems. But even if they were, and even if they came immediately after the skill and concept development, this order would reverse the natural order of learning.

This reversal is not as prevalent in teaching language as in teaching mathematics. For here, it could result in teaching a child what a dog is, by description, diagrams, and stories, and after he has learned these, then showing him a dog to test him and to make sure that he has the concept right.

6

Phase I of the Media-Action and Role-Playing Hierarchies

Real Objects, Real Actions, Real Problems

Let us look at the Natural Mathematics program and technique of teaching. The following introductory experience could take place in either a first grade or Headstart classroom.

AN EARLY SAMPLE EVENT IN NATURAL MATHEMATICS

The children are selecting bags from a box. Each bag contains two pennies and two candies. The children are not asked to group them, count them, or match them. The teacher is only telling them that they have permission to trade them, if they wish. She tells them that they will be allowed to eat the candy and put the pennies in their pockets after the trading time. "These bags are yours, and what is in them, too. But don't eat the candy or put the pennies away for a few minutes. We want to give everyone a chance to do some trading. I'll tell you when it's time."

The teacher's role is to initiate action, and if the children do not begin trading spontaneously, she takes one of the bags for herself, and offers to trade one of her candies for a penny. She holds out a candy and asks, "Does anyone want to give me a penny for this candy?" Several children come forward to trade. The teacher trades both of her candies for pennies, and tells the others they can try to trade with each other. After a few minutes, she offers to trade in reverse, pennies for candies.

The children walk freely around the room, asking others if they want to make exchanges. Paul walks over to Timmy, holding out a penny. "Give me a candy," he says.

Timmy looks at his holdings, takes out a candy, gives it to Paul, and puts Paul's penny in his bag. He walks over to the teacher and asks, "I don't have to trade if I don't want to, do I?" The teacher says that he does not. Timmy goes to his chair, sits down, rolls his bag tight and puts it on the table. He is finished. (He is not sure he really wanted to make that exchange with Paul.)

Paul moves on to talk with Rhonda. "Give me a candy," he requests. Rhonda shakes her head. Paul turns to Bill. "Give me a candy."

Bill has one candy left. He answers, "O.K., give me your penny." Paul gives Bill the penny, and takes the candy.

These exchanges are taking place without teacher instruction. The teacher moves around the room, occasionally offering to trade in either direction, to get action started where it has stopped, or to comfort a child disappointed by his inability to accomplish his wish.

The teacher has several problems. Susie lets Joe pressure her into trading both her candies for pennies; she now has all pennies and no candies. She wants her candy back, but is too shy to seek trades. She starts to cry. The teacher moves over to her and asks the class, "Susie wants a candy. Will anyone trade with her?" Mary goes to Susie and gives one to her. Susie is so upset that she takes the candy from Mary, without offering the penny in exchange. Mary reaches over and takes it. Susie breaks into tears all over again. The teacher steps into the situation with comfort and reassurance, "Don't cry, Susie, everything turned out all right. You got a candy and you traded a penny, remember?"

Joe also gets into difficulty, with Bill, who tries to take Joe's candies by grabbing for them. The teacher has all trading stop, and everyone sit down. She tells the class what happened and asks if anyone has an idea of a better way for Bill to get some candies. Mary (the philosopher of the class) asks, "Where are his pennies?"

Bill says, "I'm saving them."

Mary shakes her head. "Hmph," she says.

No one offers to give Bill a penny or a candy. The teacher says, "Too bad, Bill. No one is going to give you a candy unless you trade." Bills knocks over a chair and kicks it. The teacher turns it upright and sits him down. She says, "Think about whether you might want to trade."

Ruth has taken the wrapper off one of the candies and begins to eat it. The teacher goes to her and has her put the wrapper back on. She asks if anyone else forgot about not eating until everything was over.

After about ten minutes, trading stops. The closing requests are from children who want to buy candies. There are no sellers. The teacher makes a mental note that the next variation she selects will include an added incentive to acquire pennies, either a later "store time," or more and smaller candies, or an item not as desirable as candies. Had her particular class been more oriented toward money, she would choose a variation in the other direction.

At the end of trading time, the teacher tells the children that they can now eat the candy, or keep it, and put their pennies away. Later on, she will have a box for each child. On certain days she will require that money be saved, or that candy (or other acquired objects) be put away until after school. For the beginning, it is more important that the children be convinced by experience that the real things they are dealing with are truly theirs.

The teacher repeats the activity for several days with little variation. There are several children like Susie, who need a number of experiences of a similar pattern, before they will feel familiar and comfortable with it. Meanwhile the brighter and more adventurous children like Paul, will begin to do some advanced planning.

COMPARISON WITH TRADITIONAL LESSONS

Let us stop a moment to look briefly at some differences between this introduction and introductions in current programs, and to see how these differences affect the child:

1. The child is now solving a *real problem,* that is, a problem that is real to the child. It is also really mathematics, because it involves quantity and quantitative relationships. What makes it real to the child, however, is that it relates to his situation personally. What he does *makes a difference* in the amount of candy or money he will acquire.
2. The child is given the opportunity of *directing his own activity.* He is allowed to do whatever he wants to do, within the rules of the given situation. The teacher designs and provides the situation, and sets the rules (you can get candy by trading, but not by grabbing). The child is then free to make his own choices according to his own interests and wishes.
3. There is *action.* The child's natural mode of solving a problem is by *doing* something. He is permitted to use his natural way.
4. The action is *social.* The young child's interests are largely focused on people as well as things. The activity does not prohibit this interest. It uses it.

SUGGESTIONS FOR MORE COMPLEX VARIATIONS

We imagine that the teacher already has thought of varying the activity, by increasing the number of items and by varying the type of items (model cars, animals, dolls, marbles, jacks, hair clips, nuts and bolts, carnival trinkets, decals, etc.). By varying the items in the bags, she will keep the activity exciting. The trading, however, will remain mostly on a one-to-one ratio (one object for one penny), for some time. Occasionally, individual children try for two-to-one trades, but there is a considerable period in which the one-to-one relationship is the only quantitative exchange which is natural. This one-to-one trading ratio, initially, is independent of the outside market value of the items. It is also, initially, independent of the number of things in the bags. It is even independent of the intensity of motivation to acquire more of one thing. The child who wants most to acquire candies, for instance, will try longer to trade. But it is a slow and gradual development to the point at which he offers more than one penny for one piece.

By choosing an unbalanced content—for instance, two pennies and six mints—the teacher will implicitly encourage unbalanced trading, and accelerate its development. But the teacher will run the danger of slowing the child later, if she hurries him now by telling him that he should do it before he sees it himself. In this stage of learning, the child's natural exploration at his own pace is the important criterion.

In time, with one or two children leading the way, it will be seen that there is more than one possible trading ratio. The brighter children will initiate it and they will have a temporary advantage over the slower pupils. It takes some time for the slower pupils to grasp what is happening—even that they are "being done out of their fair share"—and more time before they realize why and how. Eventually, when they do see it, by observing themselves and others, they will adapt it to their own goals.

The bag-and-trade activity has a vast number of variations, in addition to the number and kind of items. All the bags need not contain the same things. Half the children may draw bags containing pennies; the other half, bags containing candies or other items. The number of items may be the same as the number of pennies, or different. For instance, half the bags may contain two pennies, and half, two "creepy" plastic animals; or half may contain two pennies, and the other half five jacks. Also, the split may not be half and half. Some days, for instance, all bags may contain two pennies, except for three or four which contain ten comic decals. In order to be sure that the bags are randomly distributed, the bags may be lettered, and the pupils may draw their bag by matching it to a letter card they have selected from a box.

A major variation occurs when the teacher does not have each child select a bag, but only every *pair* of children. For instance, each pair will receive a bag containing four pennies and ten snappers. In this activity, the children must divide the contents evenly, before the trading can begin. The children may solve this problem in a number of ways, depending on their individual approach. Some will divide the contents by trial-and-error counting, if they have reached the point of relating number words to objects in one-to-one correspondence sequentially, and have developed sufficient retention. At the beginning level, however, the solution will be a simple matching process—one for you, one for me, etc. Even the more advanced will regress to repeated matching if the number of items is large enough.

The teacher will have seen immediately, we imagine, that this variation suggests another entire category of problems. When the pupils become adept at a fair distribution between two, the content of the bags may be increased, and only one bag given to each three or more children.

It is obvious that these problems of distribution need not necessarily involve money. A bag to be divided between two children might contain ten jacks and no money, for instance, or two candies and four marbles. In reference to the trading-bag approach, however, we should like to mention its associations with adult buying and selling, and the social importance of money as a measure of value and a medium of exchange. It is also important to note that the majority of adult "applications" of mathematics are economic in nature. The authors will discuss their conviction of the importance of money as a teaching aid, in detail, in Chapter 14. In this connection, a later variation should include tokens (such as small flat metal discs) which are exchangeable at the rate of ten for a penny. These tokens will facilitate the introduction of large numbers, greater ease of unbalanced exchange, and, of course, lay the groundwork of experience for place value comprehension.

SHARING AS AN INTRODUCTION TO FRACTIONS

So far, the teacher has presented a sequence of activities for the children, which encourage distributions and exchanges of whole units. Sooner or later, however, she knows that the "advance to fractions" must be made. Let's say that she decides to pursue the same developmental approach. Using a design from an earlier activity, she will give kits to only half the class. But in this sharing problem, the bag will contain a single unit which must be cut or broken before it can be distributed, for instance, a bar of modeling clay. "The problem today is to make this clay go around, so that we all have the same amount to work with," is the instruction. At first, the children will simply break the bar or tear it. In this activity the teacher will direct that whichever child makes the division, the other child gets the choice of which portion to take.

This variation also presents its own sequence of complexity. A threeway division is obviously next in the social progression, although it is vastly more difficult to accomplish. (As mathematicians, we perhaps would prefer to stay with multiples of two, since they involve only repeated divisions. From the child's viewpoint, however, it is artificial to eliminate the natural sequence in favor of a concept known only to us. By allowing the difficulties to happen, we allow the child to become aware that quantities and distributions have mysterious characteristics and present real action problems.)

The last step in the developmental level of *real things* and *real actions* is the distribution of both units and parts of units, in the same problem. This type of activity would require, for instance, the division of a pack of gum among four children. By one-to-one matching, four of the sticks are distributed. By dividing the last stick into four parts and again matching one-to-one, the distribution is accomplished.

7

The Role of Language
in Phase I

MATHEMATICAL LANGUAGE DEVELOPMENT

In discussing Phase I problems, which involve *real things* and *real actions,* we have outlined the process of presenting the problem, and the action of solution by the children. We wish now to discuss the role of language. The solution of mathematical problems by symbolic language is a major goal; that is, the child's ability to solve problems by the use of numerals and operations. The child should eventually be able to *compute* with numerals; for instance, 15 cents divided among 5 children will provide each child with 3 cents.

This is the same goal which is sought by traditional mathematics programs, both old and new. Traditional programs teach skills and concepts separately from problems, with the aim of giving the child a foundation in skills and concepts, so that they may be used to solve problems later. Natural Mathematics reverses the process, using problems in order that the child may develop the skills and concepts which he will use in solving further problems.

THE EARLY INTRODUCTION OF LANGUAGE
FOR DESCRIPTION AND REFLECTION

The child will never be able to *use* the symbolic language as a *problem-solving tool,* until he becomes thoroughly familiar with it through a variety of experiences. Therefore, at every step the teacher teaches mathematical language and cultivates its use.

For instance, in the trading activity approach, the teacher will close the trading time by asking the children to sit at their desks and place the content of their bags in front of them. "Today, let's wait a minute before we put our things away, and talk about what we did." In reality, the children will already have been talking about it informally. The teacher could not have stopped them if she tried. She herself will have been talking about it with them, too. Now she is going to lead a more formal discussion. Up to this time she has been staging experiences in mathematics and social interaction. Now she will stage an experience in language arts.

She asks Joe how he came out. He answers that he has one penny, but he cannot tell her that he has six candies. The following dialogue may take place:

TEACHER: Joe, how did you come out? What do you have?

JOE: Here's what I got.

TEACHER: How many pennies is that?

JOE: One.

TEACHER: Can you tell me how many candies you have? Now everybody else stay quiet. This is Joe's business. You'll get your turn.

JOE: No, ma'am, it's this many.

TEACHER: Let's see how many that is. Put your penny down. Now put one of your candies in the other hand. That's one. Say "One." Now put another candy in that hand. That's two. Say "Two." Now put the next candy in that hand. That makes three. Say "Three." Now another one: "Four." Now another: "Five."

Now another: "Six." Now you choose someone, and ask what *he* has.

JOE: I pick John.

JOHN: I have three pennies, and I have money at home, lots of money, twenty hundred dollars.

TEACHER: John, will you hold up your three pennies so everyone can see? Who else has three pennies? Will you all hold them up? Susie, you have three pennies. Can you hold them up? All right, everybody put them down. Now, who remembers what they started with? Who has the same as when you started, just like this? Hold them up, just like I am. How will you tell somebody what you got in school today? What will you say?

SEVERAL: Two—money—candy—etc.

TEACHER: Is there anybody with all pennies? Or all candies? How many do you have? Put them on the table, and let's count as you pick them up. Pick up one and say "One." Pick up another. "Two." Pick up another. "Three," etc.

Eventually, when the children have been divided up into smaller groups, the teacher will be able to discuss with each child what he started with, what he did with it, and what he has left, so that the child uses language to re-live the activity.

The purpose of taking the child slowly and carefully through the phase of using real things, real actions, in real problems, is not that this is the "right" way to solve problems. It is vastly inferior to symbolic solutions. Its purpose is to enable the child to *acquire* the symbolic language, in such a way that it has genuine meaning. In the beginning, therefore, the language "lessons" must follow and not precede the child's activity. The words are introduced as a way of reflecting on what the child has done, and not as instructions on what he is to do.

This, of course, is the natural order of learning language. The child sees an object and then is told what it is. We do not define the object for him, and then take him to see one. This natural order is reversed so often in mathematics, because mathematics concerns events, not simple objects which can be perceived all at once. Mathematical events are very complex, involving objects, actions, distributions, equity. It is therefore far more tax-ing to the educator to create real experiences for the child in mathematics than in many other areas. That is, it is more diffi-cult to create them as a *basis* for language, without using the language as if it were already understood. As a compromise, the words are often presented first, even if they have no mean-ing, and then activities are provided which at least attempt to illustrate them. For some children, this is enough to "tie them in." But for many, it is not.

The essential point of Natural Mathematics is that the time and trouble be taken to provide the real experiences which the child needs. It is considered important that the child be able to *use* the language that he knows. His ability to learn and use more complex language depends on this foundation.

In the teaching of language, speech is introduced from the beginning of the child's life, by the normal communication of parents. It is a large jump, however, to the written symbol—either the written word or the numeral. Generally, the child has been talking for several years before he learns to read and write. The danger of separating skills from comprehension is pres-ent when the child is required to use reading or writing in advance of his ability to tie in the written symbol with its real referent. This caution does not refer to learning "to write," itself. There is no danger in learning "to count," either. The danger is present only when the child is instructed to use the symbols *as a means of solution* of problems, before the symbols have been internalized. It is here that the child becomes immo-bilized, frustrated, and alienated, when he finds himself unable to proceed. This danger is especially present in teaching mathe-matical language, because of the complexity of the mathemat-ical events which the language describes.

DRAWING AS AN EARLY FOUNDATION FOR MATHEMATICAL LANGUAGE

The authors therefore suggest that an intermediate step be used in the transition from the concrete event to the written symbols, namely, picture drawing. The drawing, like the oral discussion, is only *about* what the children have done. In Phase I, the children do not use their pictures to make any decisions or find out anything. Their pictures are purely descriptive. They serve as records. They constitute the first pencil-and-paper representation.

A child passes out paper. The children get their pencils. The teacher says, "Now that trading is over, today let's put all our things on a piece of paper, and each of you draw a picture of what you have. You can do it by drawing around each thing."

Some of the children do not draw around each item, but only around a few of them. Some of the children only draw one item; for instance, they take one of their pennies and trace it over and over. It takes time and practice before they are able to portray their holdings accurately.

Samples of drawings from 4 and 5 year olds are shown. Each child had started with either 4 pennies or 6 candy sticks. The drawings are of their final holdings. The identification of the actual number (circled) is by the teacher. One of the drawings shows numerals written by the child. At this time, it is appropriate that the child begin learning to read and write the numerical symbols, also, but only in the context of language arts.

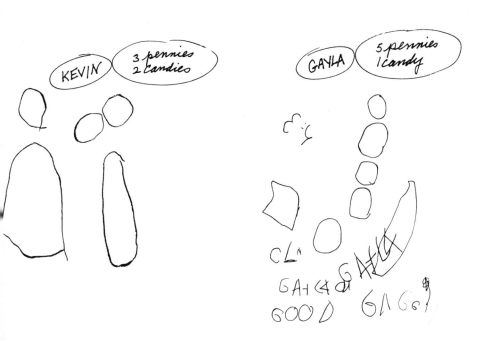

8

Integration of Reading into the Natural Mathematics Program

The authors have presented the use of mathematical language, for problem-solving, as a major goal of mathematics education. It has also been discussed that, if it is to be used as a language, its terms must be learned. The authors therefore have stressed the importance of introducing mathematical language from the outset of the mathematics program. The point of difference between Natural Mathematics, and current programs, is that mathematical language is not presented as a problem, nor as a means of solving one. It is introduced as descriptive symbols *about* the activity—just as any non-mathematical language is introduced.

In the previous chapters, a model has been offered for introducing mathematics, which is equally applicable to the introduction of reading. The key feature of the Phase I level in Natural Mathematics is that the problem be real. The key in Natural Reading is the same. The child's full potential for learning will be engaged if he is involved in a real problem.

A SAMPLE EVENT INTEGRATING READING WITH NATURAL MATHEMATICS

Learning to read by making choices

In order to utilize this potential, the teacher may add a pre-liminary activity to the bag-and-trade approach. She does not assemble the bags in advance, herself, but has each child select items according to the words on a card which the child has chosen. One version of this procedure is as follows:

The teacher sets up, on a board, as many number cards and as many word cards as there are children. The numbers range from 1 to 7. The words read either "pennies" or "candies." The teacher calls on each child in turn to come forward. The first child goes to the board and takes his pick of the word cards, and then his pick of the number cards. Suppose the child chooses "3" and "pennies." He then moves to a table on which the items are arranged. The teacher asks him what his card says, and how many. If he cannot tell, she suggests that he hold it up and see if anyone else knows what it says. If no one does, the teacher tells him. She asks him now to take the 3 pennies. If he cannot count them, he may get assistance from other members of the class. This child now has 3 pennies. He may keep his cards. It was not what he meant to choose; rather, he wanted candy. But he still has something of value; and he made his own choice. He has not been punished; and he has *discovered* what his choice meant. Furthermore, he does have the opportunity to trade for candy.

The second child may make the same reading error—or he may learn from the experience of the first child and the cards which that child chose. That is, if the next child also wants candy, he may know to pick the "other kind" of card. Or if he wants pennies, he may know to pick the same. If he does not learn from the experience of the first child, he may learn from his own. The learning of reading is accomplished by trial and error, in which the child is motivated to learn by his desire for a particular choice. The reading problem is real to the child, because it has personal consequences to him. His accuracy in word-decoding makes a difference.

In this activity, the child is learning to read numerals as well as words. However, it is important to realize that what is being learned, now, is mainly language. Other than the counting, the real problem in this activity is non-mathematical. It is a reading problem. The teacher is using language to set the conditions of the problem, as previously she used language to talk about the problem afterwards. Thus reading has been integrated with mathematics. The mathematical problem continues after the child has whatever he chooses, in his efforts to change (or keep) what he has.

Counting is also learned while the child counts out what is to be his (with the directive help of the teacher and/or pupils). Although it is intensely motivating for the child to count out what he is to receive, he is still not required to use mathematical symbols to solve a problem. He is simply learning number words, with the help of teacher and pupils, in the process of picking up what is to belong to him. In this part of the activity, he will not have any personal consequences as a result of mis-counting, since he will be corrected.

This type of activity may be started after only a few weeks, as soon as the children become accustomed to the idea of getting the bags and being free to trade their contents. The child need not be able to read the numerals, since in the counting the teacher is available as helper and director.

Since only the first several children called up may have a full choice of cards, the order of calling becomes important. Each child's turn may be determined by rotating the children's names on a card chart.

As a readiness activity preceding the experiences just described, the teacher may simplify the task of the child by using two trays, with the objects separated, and a label-card attached to each tray. The children then are not required to match the card they choose directly to the object. They are provided a transition step in which they only need to match their card with the label-card. While helpful in providing initial successes, this transition should not be prolonged. The essence of reading comprehension is the child's ability to relate the word directly to its referent (either the object or the action), and not back to itself.

In this activity, the essential feature is that each child have his chance to make a real choice of cards, and that the chance be repeated often. The importance of developing a sight vocabulary in this manner is that the child's first experiences with reading will be ones in which reading performs a functional service for him. His future attitude toward reading and school learning may well depend on its relevance to his personal motives.

Writing activities soon follow the introduction of reading, depending upon the readiness of the children. In the initial stages, it will be remembered, the children drew pictures of the items they had after trading. They continue to do this, but it has been the authors' experience that the children themselves also initiate writing the numerals and the word-names of the items. The names of the items are copied from the cards they selected, and which they are allowed to keep.

When the children have arrived at this stage, their experiences in Phase I then will include sight reading of numerals and words, counting, discussion, trading, picture drawing and writing, all within a social context which is truly child-centered. These language arts experiences, it must be remembered, accompany the problem-solving (matching, counting) experiences in that they set the stage for and describe the action. It is also important that these language arts experiences accompany the real problems, the real materials, and the real actions, because they allow the child to become familiar gradually with the nature of symbolic language, including mathematical language which he will use later *to solve problems* at the symbolic level.

The following description and dialogue is an actual account recorded in a Headstart classroom in which the authors employed the above procedures.

Words used today: oranges, apples, bananas, cookies, candies, toys, pennies, books, and crayons. Number cards were 1, 2, 3, and 4, and the children were asked to choose two number cards. The variation of two number selections by each child introduces the opportunity for functional addition.

DESSIE: I'm last. I go last today.
TEACHER: Who is first today?
CLASS: Kenneth.

Kenneth takes a "1" number card, a "4" number card, and a "books" card.

TEACHER: What do you get?
KENNETH: 5 books.

Kenneth takes 5 coloring books while counting each one.

KENNETH: 1, 2, 3, 4, 5.
TEACHER: Who is next?
CLASS: Margie.

Margie chooses a "pennies" card, a "3" card and a "4" card.

TEACHER: What do you get?
MARGIE: Pennies, 3 and 4.

Margie counts 7 pennies.

MARGIE: 1, 2, 3, 4, 5, 6, 7.
TEACHER: What do you have?
MARGIE: 7 pennies.
TEACHER: Who is next?
CLASS: Nathan.

Nathan chooses a "cookie" word card, but doesn't say the word. He chooses a "3" card and a "4" card and counts the dots on the back of the cards.

NATHAN: 1,2,3—1, 2, 3, 4.

Nathan puts a cookie on each dot and counts them. He puts them in a bag.

NATHAN: 1,2,3—1, 2, 3, 4.
TEACHER: Who is next?
CLASS: Velma.

Velma chooses a "toy" card and a "4" card and a "1" card.

TEACHER: What do you get?
VELMA: Toys, 4 and 1.

Choosing cards

Velma takes 5 toys.

TEACHER: What do you have?
VELMA: 5 toys, 1, 2, 3, 4, 5.
TEACHER: Who is next?
BRUCE: Me.

Bruce chooses a "3" card, a "1" card, and a "candies" card.

TEACHER: What do you get?
BRUCE: 4 candies.

Bruce takes 4 candies without counting verbally.

TEACHER: Who is next?
CLASS: Virnette.

Virnette chooses a "3" card, a "4" card, and an "oranges" card.

TEACHER: What do you get?
VIRNETTE: Oranges—3 and 4.

Virnette counts the oranges and puts them in a bag. She loses count when she reaches six. She looks in the bag and counts them again and adds one.

VIRNETTE: 1, 2, 3, 4, 5, 6—1, 2, 3, 4, 5, 6—. I need one more—7.
TEACHER: Who is next?
CLASS: Calvin.

Calvin takes a "1" card, a "2" card, and a "crayon" card.

TEACHER: What do you get?
CALVIN: Crayons—1 and 2.

Calvin takes 3 crayons.

CALVIN: 1, 2, 3.
VINNIE: I go next—my turn.

Vinnie chooses a "pennies" card and two "3" cards.

TEACHER: What do you get?
VINNIE: Pennies—3 and 3.

Vinnie counts out 6 pennies.

VINNIE: 1, 2, 3, 4, 5, 6 pennies. See, I can count right.
TEACHER: Danny, what do you get?

Danny chooses a "bananas" card and a "2" and a "3" card.

DANNY: Bananas, 3 and 2—5 bananas.
TEACHER: Who is next?
CLASS: Carla.

Carla chooses an "apple" card, a "2" card, and a "3" card.

Counting out items

TEACHER: What do you get?
CARLA: Apples.
TEACHER: How many apples do you get?
CARLA: 2 and 3—5.

Carla counts out 4 apples and then adds one. She puts them in a bag.

CARLA: 1, 2, 3, 4, and I need one more, 5.
DESSIE: My turn.

Dessie takes a "candies" card, a "2" card, and a "3" card.

TEACHER: What do you get?
DESSIE: Candies.
TEACHER: How many?
DESSIE: 2 and 3.

Dessie counts out 5 candies.

DESSIE: 1, 2, 3, 4, 5.
VINNIE: That's the last one. Dessie's the last one. I trade with you. I trade with you.

The teacher puts the remaining items in the box containing items which cost one penny apiece. She also brings out a box containing *larger items which cost 5 pennies apiece. This box also contains banks for children who want to save their pennies. The other children are free to play with their choices or trade with each other. A group of children gather around the table with the boxes—some wanting to trade—some just watching. Danny picks up a card of small toy planes.*

DANNY:	I got some of these at home. I play with these early in the morning and my mama comes out and says, "What in the world is that?" How much is this?
TEACHER:	How much is everything in this box?
KENNETH:	5 pennies. I need a bag.
VINNIE:	I trade with you. Hey, I trade with you.

Buying from teacher

Buying from teacher

Vinnie trades 2 pennies for 2 toys with the teacher.

Margie buys 3 coloring books, 3 toys and 1 candy from the penny box.

BRUCE: (*to Margie*) I want to see what you got.
MARGIE: Stop it with my things, boy.
BRUCE: How much is this purse?
VELMA: That's mine—give me it!

Danny buys a bracelet for a penny from his bank.

Dessie trades with Virnette, 2 candies for 2 oranges.

DESSIE: Girl, you want to trade? Hey, Velma, trade with
           me.
VELMA: Where's my book?
DESSIE: Vinnie, give me a penny.
VINNIE: No!
DESSIE: Vinnie, give me a penny.
VINNIE: No!
DESSIE: Nobody don't want to trade with me.

VIRNETTE:	Calvin, you want to trade?
CALVIN:	Naw.
BRUCE:	How much is this?
KENNETH:	That's 5 pennies.
CALVIN:	I trade, Kenneth.
KENNETH:	I don't trade.
DESSIE:	Give me a book (*to Kenneth*).
DANNY:	My bank is empty now.
KENNETH:	No.
MARGIE:	I got books, too.

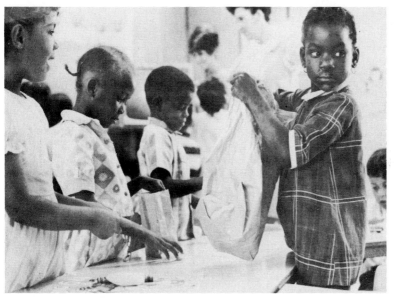

Trading with each other

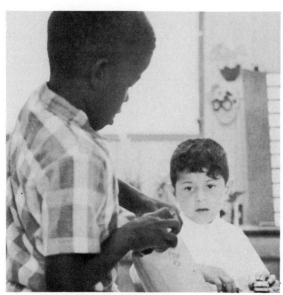

Trading with each other

PHOTO COURTESY OF SHARRON KIRELUK

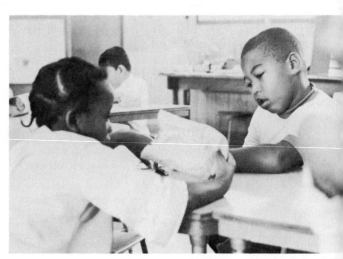

PHOTO COURTESY OF SHARRON KIRELUK

Trading with each other

At the close of the trading time, the teacher asks each child to recall what has happened. These initial experiences in reconstructing his own behavior cultivate the child's ability to reverse his own thought, which is fundamental for achievement in mathematics.

TEACHER:	Let's see what we have now. Bruce, what did you get?
BRUCE:	A monkey.
TEACHER:	A monkey?
BRUCE:	(*smiling*) Toy and candy.
TEACHER:	What did you get first?
BRUCE:	Candies — 4 candies.
TEACHER:	Now what do you have?
BRUCE:	3 candies and 1 toy.
TEACHER:	Vinnie?
VINNIE:	4 pennies and 2 toys. I had 6 pennies.
TEACHER:	Calvin, what did you get?
CALVIN:	3 crayons.
TEACHER:	What do you have now?
CALVIN:	3 crayons, I didn't trade.
TEACHER:	Virnette, what did you get?
VIRNETTE:	Oranges—8, no? 1, 2, 3, 4, 5, 6, 7—I have 7 things, candies, toys, oranges, and apples.
TEACHER:	Danny?
DANNY:	I got bananas—5 bananas. Now I have 3 bananas and 2 toys.
TEACHER:	Nathan, what did you get?
NATHAN:	(*counting cookies*) 1, 2, 3, 4, 5, 6—1, 2, 3, 4, 5, 6, 7.
TEACHER:	Dessie, what did you get?
DESSIE:	5 candies and now I got 3 candies and 2 oranges. I traded with Virnette.
TEACHER:	Kenneth, what did you get?
KENNETH:	5 books.
TEACHER:	What do you have now?
KENNETH:	5 books. I didn't want to trade.
TEACHER:	Margie?
MARGIE:	I got 7 pennies and I traded for 3 coloring books, 3 toys, and 1 candy.
TEACHER:	Carla, what did you get?

CARLA: Apples—5 apples.
TEACHER: How many do you have now?
CARLA: 3, and 2 other things.

DESSIE: I want to be teacher today.

Dessie stands in front of the class and holds up name cards and word cards. The children read the cards. Most of the children know all the words even when the cards are upside down. They tell her when she holds the cards upside down.

VINNIE: Now I want to be teacher.
VIRNETTE: I want to be teacher.
TEACHER: Danny is the second teacher.

He hides the cards behind his back to try to fool the group. The group reads the words on the cards as they go behind Danny's back.

DANNY: I can't even trick you!

Everyone is shouting when Danny finishes: I want to be teacher!

TEACHER: Let's draw what we got today.

Margie passes out paper and 2 crayons to each child. The children draw what they have.

TEACHER: If you want your name cards to write your names, I will give them to you.
KENNETH: I can't write my name. What's that? (*to Danny*)
DANNY: I don't know how to draw.
VINNIE: See what I did? (*showing her drawing*)
BRUCE: I can write my name.
VELMA: Write my name.
CARLA: Write my name.
MARGIE: I'll help you. Start right here.
KENNETH: I can't write my name.
DANNY: I can, D-a-n-n-y.
DESSIE: I don't know how to do it. Let me see your pen.
MARGIE: I want it, too!

Nathan writes his name with the crayon and then comes over to get the pen from the teacher. He waits for his turn and then writes his name with the pen.

Playing teacher

Playing teacher

Writing and drawing

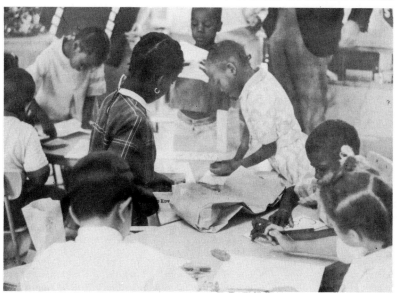

Writing and drawing

Further development of natural reading

The possibilities of the card-selection approach, for teaching reading itself, are virtually unlimited. The cards read simply "penny" or "candy." The child chooses his card, and gets what it says. When he can distinguish successfully between "penny" and "candy," a third card may be added to the selection, for instance "toys," then a fourth, fifth, etc. In subsequent variations for vocabulary extension, the broad categories of objects may be classified by specific types. For instance, the particular toy may be specified, as "jack," "marble," "soldier," etc. Plastic trucks, trains, airplanes, cars, boats, dolls, animals of all kinds (prizes may be offered for complete sets), furniture, etc., will constitute a substantial reading vocabulary. Nouns learned in this way are not limited to objects which are of value to children. Choices may involve real alternatives between objects which have value and those which have not: stick, leaf, wrapper, paper, clothespin, can, cap, bag; or between objects which have more value and those which have less: pencil, crayon, chalk, card, string, spoon, box, etc. The number of cards from which the child may choose may be increased regularly. Each child eventually may be provided with a whole deck. (The deck may finally be replaced by a list.)

Adjectives may be taught in the same way. "Red truck" or "blue truck" become the alternatives; "square cookie" or "round cookie," "tin soldier" or "plastic soldier." Prepositions indicate things "on the table" or "under the table," "in front of the door" or "behind the door." Verbs may be taught by choices of action. During play times, children card-select between "Jump rope" or "Climb the bars"; "Play ball" or "Dig in the sandpile." The class may be given the choice of being in a group which will "Sing" or "Dance," "Read" or "Draw," "Cut" or "Color."

A SAMPLE ACTIVITY INTEGRATING READING, SOCIAL STUDIES AND LANGUAGE WITH NATURAL MATHEMATICS

The entire reading activity may be advanced by allowing trading of cards. The cards also may be used as a basis for a banking system in which all properties of the children are placed in a common storehouse. The child's cards serve as a "passbook," by which he may keep account of his savings and withdraw his personal belongings during class time allotted to this activity.

The following kind of activity is an example of the possibilities for development of these experiences, in an event which reflects the coalescence of mathematics, social studies, and language arts—in the same way as they are organically fused in life. The teacher initiates:

"Today is card-trading day. Each of you has a box of things in the storehouse. You each have made cards saying how many of each item you have. John, will you read your cards?" John reads his first card. It says he has 4 trucks. One is red; one is blue; two are green.

"John, what do you need to complete your set?" John answers that he needs a yellow truck and a black one.

"Today we haven't time to get out the boxes. We'll just trade on the cards. When you make a trade, remember to change your numbers. Cross off the old one and put down the new one and write the name of whomever you traded with; and then both of you come and show me how you've done it."

For an activity of this kind, the children must be in Phase III, IV or V of the Media-Action Hierarchy (the transactions are accomplished with drawings, tally marks or numerals); but the phase on the Role-Playing Hierarchy is Phase I (the outcomes are real); and the phase on the Complexity Hierarchy is also rudimentary (the usual computation is simply the addition or subtraction of small numbers).

For this activity to take place on Phase V of the Media-Action Hierarchy, the required background is that the children have learned to count, to read and write numerals, and to read words for the objects which the children have acquired. There should have been previous trading events in which the real objects were exchanged (Phase I of the Media-Action Hierarchy) and previous trading events in which individual cards (one card for one item) were exchanged (Phase II of the Media-Action Hierarchy), and previous trading events in which the trades were accomplished through use of drawings (Phase III) and tally marks (Phase IV).

Card-trading is not only an intensely motivating and effective learning event in itself. It is a foundation on which the teacher may build more advanced socio-mathematical experiences; for instance, the class purchase of a share of stock by subscription of sub-shares.

9

Discussion and Analysis of Phase I of the Media-Action Hierarchy

REAL OBJECTS, REAL ACTIONS, REAL PROBLEMS

Let's go over what has been happening in Phase I:

The children have been manipulating concrete materials.
The children's interest has been stimulated.
The children's abilities have been challenged.
The children's participation has been enlisted.
The children have been encouraged to look for patterns.
The children have discovered for themselves.
The children have explored ideas.
The children have analyzed.
The children have been motivated to think.
The children have evaluated.
The children have inquired.
The children have advanced at their own pace.
The children have distributed things.
The children have shared things.
The children have engaged in social interaction.
The children have had real problems.
The children have had action.

The children have been allowed their own solution.

The children have rewarded themselves.

The children have been directors.

The activities have been child-centered.

The activities have appealed to the child's hedonism.

The activities have appealed to the child's egocentricity.

The children have acquired skills (and number concepts and rudimentary operations) in the process of solving a problem—not as separate techniques which later must be related to their application.

The children have acquired skills in oral and written language in the process of reflecting on what they have done and in the process of acquiring what they wish to have—not as vocabulary which later must be "tied in" with reality.

The children have been introduced to mathematics as a part of living—not as separated "learning."

WHY CURRENT PROCEDURES FAIL

Teachers of young children will have wondered why so few of the accepted "good principles" of education are successfully translated into actual practice in current mathematics programs. The authors suggest that it has been the result of a combination of difficulties, in both the circumstances of current programs and their theoretical foundation. Among the circumstantial difficulties have been overcrowded classrooms, lack of finances, and the contradictory burden placed on teachers to consider each child as an invaluable individual and yet be judged by the child's advance on standardized tests which often emphasize isolated symbolic computation. The primary difficulties in the theoretical foundation have been the insufficient attention to the developmental stages through which each child must progress and the persistence of subject-emphasis over child-emphasis. These difficulties have not been resolved, because a teaching model has not been developed which would advance a child through Piaget's developmental stages, at the same time utilizing Dewey's principles of the primacy of natural motivation in learning, through the child's involvement in his own activities.

THE ESSENTIAL FEATURE OF PHASE I

The essential feature of Phase I is that everything can be real to the child: *real things, real problems, real action.* Moving the *child* into quantitative action is the primary consideration of the teacher. Her curriculum is child-centered.

Traditional mathematics, on the other hand—both "old" and "new"—are skill- and concept-oriented. They make concessions to the child's natural interests, but they do not place primary emphasis on them. They select the skill or concept to be mastered, from a scope-and-sequence, which is based on the already known structure of mathematics. The teacher's task is then to be ingenious and acrobatic in convincing the child that he can trust it, that it is right, that it means something.

Faced with this task, the teacher may use concrete demonstrations. She may count the windows in the room, and walk around and touch each one as she counts. She may count a stack of books on her desk, moving one book over to another pile with each counting word. She may count the number of balloons in a box, holding each one up as she counts it. She may count the children in the room by pointing to them, or as she passes out a pencil to each one. In each demonstration, she emphasizes the final count by a dramatic change in her tone of voice. She uses a tone which conveys surprise or amazement or satisfaction.

Such demonstration experiences are, in fact, arguments. They are arguments that something important is happening; their point is that something important is to be learned. They are arguments that "how many" means something of importance to the child—and that he really should want to know it.

The argument is satisfying to the educator because it is education-centered. But it may not be satisfying to the child, because it is not child-centered. The child may not really participate in the argument, because it is not his; it is the teacher's, or the school's or the book's. The child is not really interested in the argument because it is not an argument about his personal life. It is a long trip from the young child's hedonism and ego-centricity to a genuine aesthetic satisfaction that the world is made of sets, numbers, or other neutral or impersonal ideas.

In the effort to give meaning to the skill, the teacher may have the children use manipulative materials themselves. For instance, she may pass out bottletops as counters. The children will then be counting concrete ("real") things, and actually moving them in the process. But again, it is a concept-centered, not a child-centered activity. Why should the young, egocentric child care if he has three or five bottletops on his desk? What difference can it really make to him? If the child's pre-school education has already motivated him to learn for learning's sake or for social approval, the learning itself will be a goal. For many children, however, such pre-school attitude formation has not occurred.

DIFFERENCE BETWEEN "CONCRETE" AND "REAL"

The difference between "concrete" and "real" is crucial, in the view of the child. The tangibility of a concrete thing, of course, makes it real in the sense that it is not make-believe. But it may have little meaning for the child in the sense that it *makes a difference.* Use of the concrete may facilitate skill learning, but still may not lead the child into interest in "outcomes." It accelerates skill-learning prior to the child's appreciation of its usefulness to him. Later, he has the familiar difficulty of relating which skill to use in solving which problem. In pedagogical terms, the child is unable to "transfer."

Thus, while real things are important, and real action is important, it is the setting of a real problem which is primary. The reality of the problem is what makes the things and the actions real *psychologically,* as well as tangibly. Tangible materials, apart from a real problem, are just as likely to distract the child as to assist him in developing the concepts they are used to illustrate.

THE TEACHER STAGES "EVENTS"

In Natural Mathematics, the teacher begins—not with the concepts or skills—but with whatever purposeful activities are of interest to the child. The teacher's task is to know what is of interest to the child, and from this, to be creative in selecting those activities which have quantitative possibilities. Her task then is to set a real, quantitative problem, to keep the action moving, to maintain fairness and tolerance, and to be patient and comforting while the child experiences the divergent results of various trials and errors of his own. In other words, she stages a real quantitative event, real from the child's own life-view.

This technique begins with the behavior of the child, and then uses language to assist the child to re-live his behavior and reverse his thoughts about it. Through language, he is able to express the common elements of his quantitative problems and categorize his behavior, so that each problem-solving experience does not remain unique, separated, and isolated from the others. Through language he develops policies for becoming efficient, for planning ahead, for describing fairness and precision. When these policies of action are stabilized and verbalized, they are called concepts. Current mathematics programs are based on the faith that logical explanations, backed by or preceded by illustrative activities and illustrative exercises, will produce such concepts more quickly and more firmly. Our present failure with many children, especially the disadvantaged, suggests that this faith is not justified. Natural Mathematics presents an approach which aims at developing, rather than reshaping, the child's natural construction of reality.

INTEGRATION OF SUBJECT AREAS

It is clear from this approach, that the authors consider learning in mathematics to be organically integrated with learning in social studies and language arts. In fact, Natural Mathematics rests on the conviction that the disciplines are inseparable in the child's natural construction of reality. The statement "1 + 1 = 2," a mathematical statement, can have no meaning for a child until he can think of 1 of something. He can accomplish this only through his growth in the language of objects. Until he has available a firmly established image of a dog, he cannot think of 2 of them, not even of 1, in the same way that he can't think of a big one or a black one.

Just as fundamental, "1 + 1 = 2" can have little meaning for the child until he *wants* to think of "1 + 1 = 2" of something. His motivation to do so is a matter of growth in social (and temporal) consciousness. As long as he is aware of himself alone and of the immediate present, of the actual and not the possible, of absolute gratification and not relative gratification, he will not be able to think of "how much" or "when," but only of "whether."

When the child's consciousness does broaden—through many experiences and his increasing reflection about them—it is a general growth, involving the total personality and ability of the child. It is not subject matters which grow in separate but parallel or interdependent fashion. The disciplines, as such, do not grow at all. Only the child's mental power grows. And as his mental power grows, he becomes more capable of "constructing" the disciplines.

The children who take a vote on what time to have games have little interest in whether the issue is classified as language arts, social studies or mathematics. They engage in all three simultaneously. Later, the child does begin to view the fields as separable in content. This view is a result of education. Of course, the child learns to distinguish the disciplines very early, in form. Each subject has a different textbook or workbook; the symbols look different; they are studied at different times of day; the teacher makes verbal distinctions which the child learns ("Time for arithmetic now"). But these distinctions are external to content, as far as the child is concerned. They are likely to inhibit growth, since they often limit the child's natural pursuits without providing compensating stimulation in the new direction. Every teacher is aware that the engrossed child is usually doing something, and usually doing it with someone. And she is aware, also, that such children are not likely to be learning a specific subject matter, but a composite by-product of a social activity.

Language arts especially is an outgrowth of social activity. If the child does not develop a desire to communicate, there is little reason for him to learn language as a means of communication. If he should learn language for some extrinsic reason, he will be less likely to use it for its desired purpose. In mathematics, the same principle holds. If a child does not develop a desire to measure, to distribute, to receive, to share equitably, there is little intrinsic reason for him to learn mathematics.

The reader is referred to Chapter 4 for a discussion of the distinctions between an exercise and a problem, and the elements of a problem which make it real to the child. It will be noted that such problems arise from situations which are social. They may or may not be presented through formal language; however, they always involve communication. In evaluating the psychological reality of a mathematics problem, in fact, its degree of integration with language and social studies may be used as a criterion. The transfer difficulty which children experience—not knowing which computational skill to use—is the direct consequence of separating one subject area from another. If the child is taught the skills of each area separately, it is not surprising that he internalizes them as separate and does not know how to cross over in "application." In Natural Mathematics, the child is offered problem-situations which necessarily maintain the natural integration of the subject areas. The child's skills and concepts grow out of his problem-solving actions, as he classifies his own behavior in these integrated events. His transfer problem has not been "solved"; rather, it has not been created.

The job of the teacher, then, is to present situations in which the child will find language and mathematics socially useful.

Eventually, of course, he will in out-of-school, everyday experiences. The educator's job is one of acceleration, so that learning may be condensed to a shorter time span than unplanned experiences would allow. This does not mean that the steps may be skipped, or that the sequential development may be abbreviated. It means that the teacher should structure the type of events which would otherwise come about naturally, but in a helter-skelter order and at widely spaced intervals. She selects a sequence of experiences which will have its foundation in the child's already-existing interests, and she designs and orders the quantitative events of the curriculum.

One such teaching procedure is the "trading" approach. Therein the child is engaged in the following activities which integrate the traditional subject matter areas:

 a. Choosing a card (reading).
 b. Counting out the objects chosen (arithmetic).
 c. Trading (arithmetic, language, socialization).
 d. Recording (arithmetic, writing).
 e. Teacher-pupil discussion, including reporting, reflection, evaluation, planning (oral language, socialization).

The "trading" approach is only one of many such events, although it may be the most dynamic, and the only one in which every child can have his own problem simultaneously.

MONEY: A UNIQUE TEACHING AID

Money has a unique usefulness in the design of a real quantitative event. It is, almost without exception, motivating to children. Children know that money buys things. They know that with money they can get things they would like to have. This is pre-school knowledge which is almost universal. When the teacher is at a loss for a motivating activity, a problem concerning the distribution or sharing of money is a reliable stand-by.

Money stimulates social interaction and communication. Its value depends not only on the child who has it, but on the values of others who will exchange something for it. It thus engages the child in dealing with social possibilities and social limitations. The child who attempts to deal unfairly is checked by the resistance of his peers, as well as by the authority of the teacher.

Money has other educative values, which often are not attributed to it. The economic well-being of every citizen depends on his country's money policies as well as his own industry and ability. Money is sometimes considered as a somewhat "low class" application of mathematics. There are a number of good mathematicians, however, who do not understand the consequences of a Federal Reserve decision to raise or lower the interest rate, or the connection between raising taxes and protecting the dollar, or how the devaluation of the dollar can lead to international depression. The factors leading to a rush on gold or sterling and the strategies to counteract it are topics of controversy at the highest level of international relations. The fact that the vast majority of citizens do not understand it at all is a commentary on the absence of real money problems in the classroom.

The authors' emphasis on money, things to eat, and things to play with, in Phase I, does not deny the possible psychological reality of early scientific inquiry, based on a child's natural curiosity. Such projects as measuring rainfall, temperatures, and plant growth are also effective activities for children. However, they presume a quantitative interest on the part of the child, and should not be imposed on him as long as his own interest is still qualitative. That is, the young child's curiosity about raindrops is not automatically convertible into interest in inches of rainfall. Nor is his wonder at sunbeams a sign of readiness to measure degrees of temperature.

For most very young children, and especially the disadvantaged, the authors believe that quantitative interests emerge mainly from "economic" problems (problems of acquisition and equitable sharing). "Scientific" interests, insofar as they are quantitative, are less intrinsic. Quantitative scientific activities are more advanced, in that they require use of objective standards of measurement and depend upon prior quantitative experiences. They also involve indirect and less immediate gratifications than activities concerning acquisition. Consequently, quantitative scientific activities may not be effective or motivating in Phase I. If they are uninteresting or too advanced, they may depress the child's positive attitude toward school-learning. If they fail to serve their purpose at the time they are undertaken, their possible effectiveness at the time when they would become really appropriate may also be reduced. Every teacher has had the experience of designing an activity which she knows is needed, only to have a child sigh, "We did that last year. Do we have to do it again?" The fact that it now will be a repetition reduces its present interest and encumbers it with negative attitudes which are carried over from the time when it lacked reality.

Phase I is characterized by this reality, in terms of the child's view of it. It is the central criterion of the program. "The child is the starting point, the center, the end. It is he and not the subject matter, which determines the quality and quantity of learning." [1]

---

[1] John Dewey, *The Child and the Curriculum*, University of Chicago Press, Chicago, Illinois, 1902.

10

Phase II of the Media-Action Hierarchy

TANGIBLE REPRESENTATIONS

This discussion of Phase II refers to Phase II of the Media-Action Hierarchy, and not necessarily to Phase II of the Role-Playing Hierarchy. It will be recalled that the Phase I discussion in the previous two chapters referred to Phase I of both hierarchies. The media and actions were real (Phase I of the Media-Action Hierarchy), and the problems were real (Phase I of the Role-Playing Hierarchy). In Phase II of the Media-Action Hierarchy, the child takes his first step away from the real. Representations will be used as substitutes for the real objects in the problems. The representations will be tangible (cut-outs, sticks, buttons, cardboard, string, etc.). The child's actions will remain real. That is, he will continue to solve his problems by physical matching, exchange, counting.

At the outset of this phase, his problems should remain real also. That is, the child should remain in Phase I of the Role-Playing Hierarchy. By using representations, he will be solving his problems in a mode one step removed from the real. His solutions will thus also be in the form of representations. However, the problems should initially remain those of acquisition, trading, and sharing, whereby he may turn in his representational solution for the "real thing."

This phase of the Media-Action Hierarchy perhaps parallels what is sometimes referred to in the history of mathematics as the "dawn of mathematics." The authors would modify this description to the "dawn of symbolic mathematics," since early man did the same mathematics when he traded horses on-the-hoof, as when he first negotiated the trade with representational substitutes. The difference lies not in the process of solution, but in the media used.

The representative mode leads to tremendous developments beyond its original purpose: record-keeping, new notation, new language, solutions in advance, prediction, science, economics, and all their interrelations. Perhaps the most important consequence of the representational mode is the possibilities it opens for the solution of hypothetical problems. For the purposes of the education of children, this advance is crucial. The hypothetical possibility allows the child to learn prior to the event, and provides the opportunity for a greater variety of problem-solving experiences.

To the educated adult, Phase II (tangible representations) may superficially seem a mere bridge between Phase I (the real) and Phase III (picture drawing). To the child in the process of development, however, it is one of the most important steps he takes. We therefore urge that it be allocated its deserved portion of classroom time and teacher energy and training. When the child has learned to solve distribution problems with real money, real candy, real clay, similar problems should be solved with representations. That this is repetition from the viewpoint of mathematics is obvious. However, since this is the child's first experience in substituting something in place of the real in the solution of mathematics problems, it is a crucial stage in his sequential development toward use of more sophisticated symbolic substitutions. What *we* see is that the substitutions serve as well as the real, for the purpose of solution. This is what the child has yet to learn.

It is helpful, therefore, to introduce Phase II with picture cut-outs which retain the visual image of the real, but can be moved and traded. These representations are soon replaced by arbitrary objects (sticks, buttons, etc.), which do not resemble the real except for tangibility and one-to-one correspondence. The key progression in Phase II is the commencement of abstraction of the real media, with retention of their tangibility so that they still may be moved about by the child.

COUNTING AND LANGUAGE

Since language-learning accompanies problem-solving, the child will have learned to count beginning in Phase I. His counting in Phase I is descriptive, as it is in Phase II. This is the major criterion for the value of counting in Phases I and II. The neutrality of the representations which are eventually used in Phase II do not alter this criterion. Although the representations are neutral (sticks, buttons, etc.), in Natural Mathematics they always stand for something of meaning to the child. Thus, in the early phases, Natural Mathematics emphasizes counting as language to describe something which *the child wants to describe*. At least this must be its primary purpose if we want him eventually to be able to use it to solve problems. In other words, the child's orientation should consistently be toward solving problems which he perceives as having meaning (on whatever sense of meaning *he* is operating), and counting should serve him in talking about it.

INTRODUCTION OF THE HYPOTHETICAL

Phase II presents the first opportunity for the child to deal with hypothetical problems. As long as the child is working with real objects, his outcomes, too, are almost necessarily real. It would be sadistic to have a child divide a chocolate bar with three others, and then take the pieces away from them. Once the child has begun to use representations, however, no denial is necessary, since no acquisition is implied unless the teacher specifies it. Thus, the advance to Phase II of the Role-Playing Hierarchy becomes possible. This is the role-playing phase on which the child solves hypothetical variations of real problems which he has already solved. His methods of solution are the same, but he no longer keeps the outcome. These are problems of the nature, "Let's suppose that you had started with ten pennies and only one lollipop. Let's see what you would have done. Here are some pretend-lollipops and here are the pennies, only it's play money."

PLAY MONEY

Play money is an important representation in Phase II. It is perceptually very similar to real money (color, size and shape), and it allows for hypothetical problems involving larger amounts than practical with real money. It also allows for extended use of alternate forms for equivalent value (quarters, half-dollars, dollars). The teacher may display the equivalences on a flannel board, in order that the children may use them, if they wish, to solve the hypothetical problem at hand.

While the child is in Phase II of the Media-Action Hierarchy, he may even go on to Phase III of the Role-Playing Hierarchy, the acting out of hypothetical problems of adults he knows. For example, using play money, he may make hypothetical grocery purchases (play store). However, he should regularly return to real problems in order that the representations do not sever the child's identification with his activities. It is the authors' opinion that in current practices the child's role in problems or mathematics activities is usually guided not so much by the child's readiness to identify with the problem, as by the problem's mathematical content.

RUDIMENTARY MEASUREMENT

Rudimentary measurement is also an important activity in Phase II of the Media-Action Hierarchy. The problems of partition in Phase II (for instance, dividing a bar of clay) involve representations which are themselves "measured," in the sense that their size must match the size of the real object. If the child wishes to divide the clay evenly and accurately in Phase II, he makes a paper pattern by tracing or outlining, and works out his trial-and-error solution with the paper instead of the clay itself.

The degree of abstraction involved in simple measurement is not always obvious. It may be indicated, however, by the following observation: partition of a bar of clay can be accomplished with a representation which duplicates the size of the real bar in only one dimension—provided the child does the dividing along the opposite dimension. For instance, suppose the child plans to divide the bar of clay by a cut across its smaller dimension ("width"):

There is no mathematical reason to divide it this way. Indeed, in the traditional-modern presentation of fractions, it is often stressed that geometric figures may be divided in half in a number of ways:

The child could divide the bar lengthwise as well:

The child does not, however, select this dimension for cutting, because that is not how he does divide small rectangles. He divides them by holding one end in each hand, as he would hold a candy stick, and breaks it. He is not led to this method by the concept that the break across the small dimension means a smaller or more accurate line of division. He does it this way because it conforms to the way his hands and arms are best able to accomplish it.

The point is that if the child is going to cut or break the bar along its width, his pattern needs to be accurate only in length. Through experience, the child will learn this.

It should be noted that the use of measurement is unnecessary in problems involving only multiple unit matching (the exchange of "wholes"). It is unnecessary whether the child exchanges the real objects in Phase I, or their representations in Phases II, III, or IV. The representations of whole units are independent of their size: a small button will represent a peppermint as suitably as a large button, in Phase II. In Phase III, a small drawing of a boy is as accurate as a large drawing. In Phase IV, a tally mark may be any size.

Measured representations may also be used in Phase II as tangible and transportable records, for buying and making things. Using string or other unmarked representations, children may measure off lengths for hairbands, belts, jump ropes, etc. Personal measurements are also appropriate in this phase: height, waist, foot, broad jump.

From the child's point of view, the very idea of a dimension such as length is a sophisticated abstraction from the real. It is a conceptual development, not an a priori reality. Measurement presupposes a grasp of the dimension being measured, and thus assumes that this development has already taken place. The assumption is independent of the simplicity or complexity of the measurement device used. For instance, a piece of string which "just goes around" a child's waist may be a representation of his waist. But so is a piece of string which is twice as long or half as long. The teacher only needs to tie the ends in a knot, so that the string is "round" just as the child's waist is "round." That one string is longer than the other may not be seen by the child as a relevant distinction. (In fact, the string of incorrect length will appear the better representation if its ends are tied, than will the string of correct length laid out straight.) Size becomes relevant only as the child deals with it actively and pragmatically in solving problems. For this reason, the sharing problems in Phase II have special importance in the sequential development.

To impose the idea of a standardized unit of linear measurement adds substantially to the abstraction. It is sometimes hoped that the concept of a standardized unit can be made more "real," by having children measure lengths with their feet or hands. That is, the child is asked to count the number of his steps across the room, or the number of his hand-widths across the desk. It is thus demonstrated that different children have different counts, and this demonstration is used to justify acceptance of a universal, although arbitrary, standard. The problem with these activities and their explanations is that the child may see no reason for any of it. He may not be interested in standardizing the measurement because he may not be interested in the measurement in the first place. Again, the sharing problems of Phase II involve his active engagement in rudimentary measuring, out of which the concept of measurement can evolve as a categorization of his own behavior.

Measurement of weight is less appropriate in Phase II. In addition to all the abstractions involved in measurement of spatial dimensions, the concept of weight involves the measurement of an action (gravitational force).

The key advance in Phase II is from the real object to its tangible representation. Actions remain real. Problems initially remain real, but may become hypothetical. While the process of partition involves rudimentary measurement (patterns), the primary theme of Phase II is the child's acceptance of neutral representations in problem-solving. Language (numerals) remains purely descriptive.

11

Phases III and IV
of the Media- Action Hierarchy

INTANGIBLE REPRESENTATIONS: PICTURE DRAWING,
TALLY MARKS

To this point the children have been dealing with tangible objects—the real in Phase I and tangible representations in Phase II. The action of problem-solving has been real action, in which the children physically manipulate either the objects or their representations. It has been suggested that these developmental phases are those customarily neglected. It has been proposed that this gap in the child's experience is often the cause of his later "loss of contact" with mathematics.

ADVANCE SOLUTION

Eventually, however, the child will be required to solve problems which involve materials and amounts that simply cannot be introduced into the classroom. This necessity arises from both space and cost, as well as time, limitations. While it is true that many problems theoretically *could* be solved by the modes of Phases I or II, the main usefulness of more sophisticated mathematics lies in solving problems more efficiently and solving them in advance.

Let's choose a problem which does require an advance solution. Suppose it is one week before Easter. The teacher has decided to give the children a party as her treat. She announces that at the party they will have ice cream and cookies. She holds up an empty pint carton of ice cream and asks the children to discuss how many of them it would serve. They decide that it will be enough for four children. The teacher says, "Let's think about that—one of these filled with ice cream will be enough for four of you. Let's try to find out how many pints of ice cream we will have to buy. Does anyone have an idea?"

This type of problem and many others of like nature, that is, "real problems," have been solved previously in Phases I and II. The children have acted out the problems with the real elements or substitutes, so they are familiar with the "acting out" procedure. We may therefore expect that one of the children will suggest, for example, "Let's pretend we're having a party now and let's get together." If the teacher receives this response, she and the pupil will discuss what he means by "get together." By previous practice, "getting together" means that the children should get together just as they would at the party to eat the ice cream, in groups of four. If a pupil does not suggest it, the teacher reminds them of what they have done previously.

On this occasion, however, the teacher would continue, "That's a fine idea, and that's usually what we do, isn't it? Today, let's do something different. Let's see if we can draw our problem on paper."

SAMPLE PROCEDURE

Throughout Phases I and II the children have been drawing the elements of their real problems, as a part of language arts. But they have always done the drawings *after* the solution of the problem, rather than using drawing to *solve* a problem.

This time the teacher says, "Let's draw everything in the problem on paper. Let's have the boys draw the boys and the pints of ice cream they will need, and the girls draw the girls and the ice cream they will need." (The teacher may divide the class in this manner so that they will not have to draw so many children and so that there will be two problems.)

The teacher moves around the room seeing that the children are able to grasp the drawing problem. There are 33 children enrolled in the class, 20 boys and 13 girls. Today, however, three boys and one girl are absent and the teacher reminds the children to be sure to add these to the drawings so that there will be enough ice cream for the total class at the party.

The drawing action and solution of the problem for the boys may look like the following:

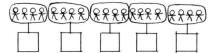

And for the girls:

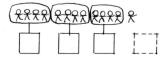

There were no boys "left over" in the problem, but the girls need three pints of ice cream with one girl left over. After some discussion it was decided that the teacher had not been accounted for and that perhaps the class could invite two guests. Therefore the girls would need four pints.

As a check for accuracy of the solution to these problems the teacher allows the children to "regress" to the acting out level by taking the pupil's suggestion and grouping themselves in clusters of four for the purpose of sharing a pint of ice cream.

Individual children check their picture-answers and the teacher leads the language arts portion of the activity by asking questions as to what each child did and to the relative merits of the two procedures for solving the same problem.

The children have now had their first problem-solving experience at the Phase III level: Picture Drawing. At this phase the children leave the three-dimensional world of objects and represent the objects by simple drawings. They also represent the action by drawings of the action: lines, circles, arrows, etc. This is the first time the children have been *required to solve* problems without the use of objects or tangible representations.

The details of the drawings will be an individual matter, depending upon both the child's ability to draw and his personal choice of varying degrees of realism. It should be remembered that the children have used drawings in Phases I and II to recreate and talk about the elements of the problems. That is, during Phases I and II the teacher has been helping the child "visualize" the problem and its solution—after he has solved it—by having him represent the objects on paper. During that time many of the children will have learned the short-cut of making very simple drawings, and even marks, to signify elements of the problem, things and people. In other words, they will have come a long way in representational drawing before they are required to use this technique to *solve* a problem.

Phase III does not represent much of a time saver in terms of solving problems. In fact, problems involving large numbers of elements must be reduced for Phase III, in order that the children do not get bogged down in the drawing itself. But it allows for solving problems which must be planned in advance. It will also allow the child to solve problems whose elements (or their tangible representations) are too bulky or are unavailable. But most importantly, Phase III allows the child to take another step away from the tangible, concrete, real world. The real world has been further internalized and he may now behave toward the drawings as he had behaved toward the real things, or their tangible representations. With the teacher's guidance, he has acquired a more sophisticated tool for solving problems.

DRAWINGS GRADUALLY BECOME NEUTRAL MARKS

Once again it must be emphasized that a major goal is the solution of problems by the use of abstract symbols and operations. Stated more simply, the goal is that mathematical problems be solved by the use of language rather than by the use of the real objects. Language in this sense is the ultimate short-cut, the short-hand of the problem solver. In the final step before the use of symbols, the drawings gradually become more abstract. The child's drawings become increasingly simplified, as he sees that his actions are not influenced by their elaboration.

Furthermore, the initial interest of the child in the details of his representation will yield to interest in efficiency, once the representation must be copied a number of times in order to match all the elements. Eventually, the drawings become neutral marks with little or no resemblance to the real. A child's drawing may progress toward the abstract in the following manner:

Phase IV is thus a gradual abstraction of Phase III, with no principle difference involved. In both phases, the crucial advance from physical manipulation to representative action (lines, arrows, circles, etc.) is maintained.

12

Phase V of the Media-Action Hierarchy

Symbolic Numerals and Computation

In the first four phases of development, the child has been learning numerals as language arts, both spoken and written. He can count up to a numeral ("How many are there?"), and he can translate from a numeral back to a collection ("Take five.") The common denominator of these phases has been the use of numerals only for the purpose of description. The child has not used numerals as a short-cut in the solution of problems.

THE USE OF MATHEMATICAL LANGUAGE
TO SOLVE PROBLEMS

In the Phase III solution described in the previous chapter— to find the number of pints of ice cream needed for the class party—the answer is most efficiently stored as a numeral, although the picture drawing is just as conclusive.

In the process of solution, the child will also have used numerals to describe the elements of the problem or to discuss them. For example, the children decide, in posing the problem, that "one" pint of ice cream is enough for "four" children. By Phase III, the children will be proficient in counting, and numerals will safely simplify the description of the problem, so long as they are not utilized to solve it.

Numerals may also be used in discussing just what the elements of the problem really are. For instance, the teacher and children will have discussed what to do about the children who are absent on the day the problem is solved. If they decide to include these children, they will provide for them by drawing representations for them as if they were there, one for each absentee. Many children will simply make "three more" representations, without the process of one-to-one identification. The *solution* will still be the drawing of the ice cream boxes, one for each group of four children. The picture so drawn provides a record of the solution. This record may then be translated into a numerical "answer," but this translation is not the solution.

During Phase III, the children will be using *written* numerals, alongside their drawings, to summarize the steps of the solution as well as the final solution. For instance, if the solution emerges from repeated drawing of groups of four pupils, the children will gradually begin labeling each group with the numeral "4." Until this time, the teacher has been helping the child with oral and written numerals, which correspond to the real objects and the drawings. Thus, within the language arts portion of the program, the child from the very beginning of his problem-solving experiences also has parallel experiences in both oral and written language relating to the problems.

During the advanced stages of Phase IV, this language gradually will begin to *replace* some of the pictures and tally marks. If the solution of a problem requires drawing a group of four pupils five times, the child may draw two such groups, label each group with the numeral "4," and decide to substitute this numeral alone for the last three groups of drawings. He may do this because by now the drawing has become repetitious and tiresome; or he may do it because he desires to arrive at his solution more efficiently. The larger the number of elements in the problem, the more incentive he will have to begin this substitution.

Through these coordinated experiences the child begins to develop certain skills and concepts which have grown out of the actual solving of the problems *and the language* he uses to represent the elements of the problem. Now in Phase V, the child takes the final step of the developmental sequence, and commences to *use that language to solve the problem.*

VISUALIZATION

In Phase V, the child is now freed from any perceptual re-production of the elements and action of the problem. These elements have become sufficiently internalized to allow him to substitute computation for counting. In other words, he is now able to visualize the problem without the necessity of any representation. He visualizes the first group of four children and the first ice cream box he would draw, and he is able to visualize them because he has solved many problems in the real and representational phases. He may visualize the second group of children and the second ice cream box also. This vis-ualization is what a teacher means when she asks children to "think" about a problem before they start "working it." But if children have not been advanced through a developmental se-quence, they do not know what to "think" about. The child who does know what to think about (his own previous problem-solv-ing-actions) "sees" the problem, because he *has* seen it. He knows that the action is the grouping of 20 boys into groups of 4, and that the numerical answer will be the number of times he has to do this in order to take care of all 20, that is, the number of times "4 goes into 20." If he has developed the meaning of numbers and operations by such experiences in problem-solving, he will know (*a*) that the operation to use is division, although he may not name it, (*b*) what to divide by what, (*c*) the result of the computation, and (*d*) to which element of the problem the answer refers. His own images will select the computer key and will remain the context of the computation, even if he puts them aside during the actual computation. The child becomes the self-programming computer.

Not all children will be able to move into this phase with the same amount of experience. Bright children will have gradually moved into this phase after fewer experiences than needed by slower children. They may have entered it without teacher guidance. For some time, all children will have been working in their own ability groups. However, at this time, it becomes imperative that the advanced children work separately from the pupils who have not yet reached this stage. For the advanced children, unnecessary repetition of Phases I–IV problem-solving procedures may become a tiresome depressant. For the others, the work of the advanced group may cause them to devalue and lose interest in the experiences they are still having, and which they still need. The concepts of *every* child should grow out of his categorization of his own behavior. To attempt to accelerate concept formation by bypassing or omitting its substance is self-defeating and child-defeating.

In review, the child initially categorizes his behavior in dealing with things; that is, he "thinks" in terms of things; then he categorizes his behavior in dealing with representations; that is, he "thinks" in terms of representations; finally, on the Phase V level, he categorizes his behavior in dealing with symbols; that is, he "thinks" in terms of symbols, or symbolically. His readiness for advanced work has truly been accomplished; the foundation is there; he is now better able to appreciate and participate in the structure of mathematics.

The earlier phases continue to retain their importance as an avenue of regression to a less abstract level, enabling the child to better visualize the elements of different problems. The regression levels are often of essential importance when a child has tentatively advanced to Phase V for a particular type of problem, but thereafter "loses his connection" with the action which is symbolized by the computations. One of the authors recollects difficulty in proving the theorem, "Let X, Y and Z be spaces, and let f: $X \rightarrow Y$ and g: $Y \rightarrow Z$. If f is continuous, onto and either open or closed, and if g $\circ$ f is continuous, then g is continuous." At this level of mathematics, abstractions should be psychologically real. Nevertheless, the author's difficulty with this theorem was resolved only after the use of a picture drawing. If a regression to Phase III is helpful for learning at this level, it is tragic for fifth graders to feel that it's a waste of time, baby-stuff, and that they can learn without it.

The major theme of the progression to Phase V is that skills and concepts have remained integrated with the child's problem-solving. Skills have been developed in the process of problem-solving; concepts have emerged from the child's self-observation. To what extent they may be separated safely, after the child is working in Phase V, depends on the child. If he views skill-exercises as satisfying tool-sharpeners, for the purpose of increased adeptness in problem-solving, he is probably not endangered by considerable separation. But if he views skill-exercises as an easier, more pleasant, unthreatening activity, whereas he views "problems" as difficult, hateful, and frustrating, we can suspect that the separation was too soon and too abrupt. For if the skills remain isolated and untransferable, they will not be relevant to the child's construction of reality.

PART 2

General Discussion, Implications, and Suggestions

13

Natural Mathematics:
An Alternative
Between "Old" and "New"

The transition from "old math" to "new math" dates to at least 1935, as a changing trend in pedagogical theory. It was given dramatic public endorsement in 1957, the year of the first Russian Sputnik.

In the old practices, the goal was skill in computation and the recognition of style of similar problems. This theory led to emphasis on drill, rote, and review by repetition. It also led to the treatment of mathematics as a catalogue of progressively more difficult skills.

Students often gained a high level of computational proficiency under these methods of teaching. Many parents today question the fact that their children bring home accounts of bundling popsicle sticks in tens, and speak of "40" as "four tens," but cannot answer immediately and surely the question, "How much is 9×6?" Parents are right when they claim that, for the purpose of learning "tables," the old methods were, and are, superior. However, the parent who recommends the old methods for teaching the skills that were useful in the old days may not be recognizing that old skills are no longer as in demand as they were. Calculating machines do much of the computing which used to be a marketable human skill. Institutions, businesses, and government provide tables of insurance premiums, interest payments, taxes, conversions of all kinds. They often provide personal consultant services to explain the tables as the need arises. Pre-digested price information is provided in stores and advertisements. Recipes on packages are shown in several columns according to the number of people to be served.

NEW ROLE OF MATHEMATICS

The pragmatic value of education in mathematics today is expanding in another direction. What the mathematics-user needs to know, now as formerly, is not just how to find the answers, but how to interpret and evaluate them. Is $1,000,000 added to the national budget a large increase? Are 50,000 auto deaths more or less than last year's rate—per driver, per car or per mile? What is an appropriate insurance plan in relation to other family needs? These are largely social judgments which are posed in mathematical terms. The possibility of government by consent depends on common understandings of the problems and of the solutions offered. As society becomes more complex, many problems and solutions will be presented increasingly often in increasingly difficult mathematical language, because no other language can symbolize them.

The professional mathematician is also required to make new uses of mathematics. At the beginning of the century, the major mathematical profession was teaching. A large number of today's professional mathematicians work in science laboratories, industry, business, and government. They are working daily with problems which must be solved through the use of mathematics. One such problem may serve as an illustration. Suppose a manufacturer has three different warehouses in different parts of the world. He receives an order from two different markets, also in different parts of the world. He knows how much he has in each of his warehouses, and he knows the transportation rates from each of the warehouses to each of the markets. He needs to know how to fill these two orders with the smallest possible transportation costs. If he has reasons for not wishing to deplete any of his warehouses, he wishes to know what alternate amounts to each market from each warehouse will still provide a profit, although a lesser one. One would think that a bit of arithmetic should give the solutions to such problems. But one finds that advanced mathematical concepts and skills are required for their solution.[1]

Other problems concern space programs: re-entry speeds of rockets as related to heat resistance of materials; economic programs: factors revelant to population growth as it relates to food production, etc. More and more, the emphasis is on the range of possible choices.

THE EMERGENCE OF "NEW MATH" IN THE TEACHING OF CHILDREN

Leading mathematicians, chemists, and physicists, as well as economists, sociologists, and biologists, deplored the graduation of college students who were proficient in outdated requirements of mathematics, but needed several years of postgraduate work in order to perform the currently required functions. They called for a reformation of mathematics instruction. They urged a shift of emphasis toward comprehension of concepts. They even urged that emphasis on particular concepts be replaced by emphasis on the integration of concepts as a logical postulate-based structure.

Paul C. Rosenbloom, Director of the Minnesota School Mathematical Center at the University of Minnesota, writes, "We have a unique problem: our society changes so fast that we can no longer predict what an adult should know and then teach this to children. . . . To prepare for a changing world, a child must learn to deal with problems for which he has not been

---

[1] G. Baley Price, *Progress in Mathematics and Its Implication for the Schools,* The Revolution in School Mathematics, National Council of Teachers of Mathematics, Washington, 1961.

specifically instructed." [2] Arden Frandsen states the same cir-
cumstance, "Difficult new problems both in school and out
of school present themselves day by day. For these novel problems there can be no adequate prepared-in-advance solution—
only an effective problem-solving approach." [3] These statements
apply to non-professional and professional users of mathematics
alike. Few disagreed with these statements. A reformation of
teaching techniques was indeed needed.

"OLD MATH," SKILL-ORIENTED; "NEW MATH," CONCEPT-ORIENTED

But as we agree that the "old math" no longer suits educational goals, we disagree that the "new math" by itself can
accomplish them. Both the "old math" and the "new math"
often do not utilize what we know about the motivational and
conceptual development of children. The "old math," with its
emphasis on algorithms (what you do to get the right answer),
rote, and repetition, rarely had personal meaning to the child.
To be meaningful to a child (as well as an adult), an activity
must enable the child to identify himself with it. That is, the
child must see himself in what he is doing. He must feel that
he is changing something, or being changed by something, that
he has evidence of his own presence; in short, that he has motive. The "old math" provided very meager opportunity for this
sense of identification. The best possible image the child could
have of himself, in relation to the mathematics, was as a competent performer. His performance could have little meaning
in itself; its meaning was almost entirely dependent on external
recognition.

The "new math," on the other hand, often de-emphasizes
the particular to the point of implying that *only* the generalizations—the concepts—are really useful. As soon as a child per-

---

[2] Paul C. Rosenbloom, "Reform in Mathematics Is Fundamental," *Mathe-matics Teacher*, March, 1964.

[3] Arden N. Frandsen, *Educational Psychology*, McGraw-Hill Book Co., Inc., New York, 1961.

forms several demonstration exercises, he is asked, "Now look what this leads to," or "Can any of you see what pattern we have here?" It is implied that what the child did so far is not in itself important, but that it was a pedagogic device to lead him to the next step. If the child is not resigned to this treatment he may hold on to his specific achievement with the particular and reject the concept.

Although the methods of modern mathematics also recognize that children must have experiences in solving problems, and that they must relate to these experiences, the practice of supplying these experiences only before, or after, the skills and concepts have been introduced persists. Problem-solving experiences suggested to the teacher are often real (such as making desserts, planning trips, distance throwing, etc.). However, these experiences are used as enrichment, either in advance, for the purpose of motivating the child by showing him an application, or later, for the purpose of illustrating the concepts involved and how they may be applied.

By serving as enrichment activities rather than as priorities, these experiences are too often neglected or relegated to the role of concessions to the child's needs. Since they are not the central, continuing content of the program, they are not available as the substance from which the child may categorize his own problem-solving actions and thus formulate concepts.

Both the "old math" and "new math" may thus miss the point that a child's experience must be his own, if it is to have true educative effectiveness.

The "old math" denies him identification, because it aims at skills. The "new math" denies him identification, because it aims at concepts. They both consider the child's experience as merely a stepping-stone to something else. What we are proposing as an alternative, Natural Mathematics, considers the child's experiences as primary, and both skills and concepts as outcomes, by-products.

14

Mathematics as Social Action

MATHEMATICS FOR EQUITY AND FAIRNESS

Mathematics is generally thought of as either a rather narrow, specialized set of rules and computations, or as a structure of formalized concepts. However, mathematics is used in people's daily affairs to earn money, to build motels, skyscrapers, bridges, to heal, to distribute and redistribute wealth, and to be precise and fair in our dealings with others. Fairness, or a good bargain by both parties, is essential to commerce. Mathematics is used as a method of arriving at a consensus of the bargainers. In short, we use mathematics, or the distribution and redistribution of things (and money especially), in social and personal interaction.

In this sense, mathematics in our everyday world is a medium of social intercourse. The natural experience of it is in a social context. It therefore should be a part of Natural Social Studies. Only in school is mathematics viewed as a separate subject, isolated from that which may "move" the child: his social values, and his immediate needs.

The authors have attempted to permit mathematics to remain in its social context, with respect to the child. The young child's view of the world is especially egocentric. Mathematics must serve his social purpose. If it does, mathematics may become a socializing influence, unseparated from the social urgencies of his life and the social life around him of which he is a part.

MONEY AS THE REPRESENTATION OF DISTRIBUTION OF REAL PROPERTY

A great majority of the time adults use mathematics in their daily lives, outside of their job, they are involved in social problems which have to do with money. It is not necessary to dwell upon the social significance of money. Ideas of free enterprise, capitalism, socialism, democracy, etc. have little meaning without the concept of property, and money is the representation of the social distribution of property. In a society in which most things are owned by someone, or some group, money becomes the representation of value of many material goods. Money then becomes symbolic of need fulfillment or may become a motivating force in itself. Even personal ethics has much to do with the tension between the utilitarian and the compulsive response to money.

Profit, loss, wages, buying, selling, debt, social security, etc. all have to do with distributions of money. They demand precision, or social equity, or justice, in terms of the values of the society. In this sense, money reflects social ethical values. The manipulation of money is thus an activity in which value, and the judgment which the word implies, is of equal importance to the accuracy of the calculation of it.

MONEY IN THE CLASSROOM

If education is to prepare individuals to live satisfying adult lives; if most adult mathematical use involves money; if a part of social intelligence is a sophisticated attitude toward the value of money, which includes a knowledge of what money will do and what it will not do, what it will buy and what it will not buy; if social ethics are involved in the distribution of money; then one has a compelling argument for the use of money in any classroom. It is motivating; children enjoy handling it; it represents value; it stimulates social intercourse; it is uniform, interchangeable, real. For the economically disadvantaged particularly, whose experience with money at home is frequently unplanned and unorganized, money in the classroom is especially effective.

SPECIAL TEACHING CHARACTERISTICS OF MONEY

Money also has a unique value in the transition from concrete to abstract media. Money is concrete in that it is tangible and has the perceptual properties of color, shape, and sound as well as texture. Money is psychologically concrete, also. It is almost impossible that a child could be reared within a family structure, without awareness of money's influence and instrumentality in his well-being and purposes.

Money is also representational in that it measures—that is, represents—units of value. Money is abstract in that it is uniform and interchangeable, has none of the perceptual properties of the objects for which it can be exchanged, nor of the social actions involved in their distribution. It is psychologically abstract because it is not an object like other objects, to be used directly or in modified form, but is used solely for exchange.

Thus the child dealing with money is spanning the concrete to abstract continuum. In a sense, he is experiencing the concrete properties of money itself, and its symbolic function simultaneously. He is on the threshold of mathematical action whenever he has money in his hands. He engages in mathematical action as soon as he participates in an exchange or redistribution. These considerations suggest that we should not use integers, fractions, decimals, and percents to teach about money, but that we should use money to teach about integers, fractions, decimals, and percents.

15

Mathematics as Distributions

Mathematics concerns the distribution of things. In one sense, mathematics may be regarded as the restructuring and distribution of one set of objects to another. The distribution may be to a set of places, e.g., a wastebasket for each room; or to a set of persons, e.g., a bag of apples for a group of children; or to a set of containers, e.g., a field of strawberries into cartons. The distribution may also take place over time, e.g., a pint of milk a day. In a time distribution, time is considered to be made up of discrete intervals. These intervals are convenient divisions of certain empirical consequences of the earth's rotation and orbit around the sun (sunrise-sunset, seasons). And the intervals, within their limits, are treated as if they were objects. The distributions may also be spatial. In this case, space is similarly considered to be made up of discrete intervals.

The notion of "relation" or "relationship" is more commonly used in mathematical discussions than the term "distribution." But relations cannot be perceived either as objects or events. Relations *describe* distributions; they tell something about how the distribution will turn out, or did turn out, in comparison to other distributions.

HOW MATHEMATICS TREATS OBJECTS AS INTERCHANGEABLE

Mathematics is concerned with the quantitative rather than the qualitative. The questions "How much?" "How many?" treat real objects as interchangeable, having no incomparable identity of their own. The discernment of common characteristics among objects (sets) places a filter over their separate identity, and regards these objects as of like value in a given respect. This regard is the enabling clause for counting, in the elementary grades; for algebra, in the secondary grades; for calculus and the study of postulational systems, at the higher levels. At every level, it thereby subjugates individual identity to classes.

QUANTITATIVE VERSUS QUALITATIVE REALITY

For the development and use of quantitative concepts, this disregard of identity is necessary. But to assume that the young child is naturally motivated to suspend temporarily his qualitative view of the world, for a quantitative one, is assuming that he has already been taught the necessity for this suspension. An even greater danger is implying the superior value of mathematics *over* the real world. A life lived by this kind of "rational beauty" might turn out to be very unbeautiful, without compassion, art or liberty. We certainly should not feel apologetic about introducing quantitative symbols. On the other hand, we are on firm educational and philosophical ground if we are respectful in introducing them as additions to, not replacements of, the qualitative reality.

DUPLICATION AND PARTITION

Another implication of the distribution view is that mathematics concerns duplication and partition. Duplication is effected by the operations of addition and multiplication, partition by subtraction and division, of elements. This Natural Mathematics model for viewing the experience of the child differs from the customary mathematical view that addition-and-subtraction, and multiplication-and-division, are simply inverse operations, although within the structure of mathematics the latter view is, of course, valid. Natural Mathematics gives priority to the problem-solving strategies of the child who is distributing; he can achieve a larger distribution by adding units to the existing one (addition), or by repetition of the entire distribution (multiplication); he can achieve a redistribution over a larger set by taking units away from the existing one (subtraction), or by partition of the entire distribution (division).

Partition, as well as duplication, disregards intrinsic identities. 2/3 of an apple is not an apple at all; in a sense, it is an ontological contradiction. It acquires meaning only as a distribution action. The child can be asked to buy the fantasy only if he wants some.

A MODEL FOR RATIONAL NUMBERS

A number itself may be considered to stand for a distribution. In order to experience a plurality such as 7 apples, a child must have moved them about, or directed someone else to move them. That is, he must have experienced the action of distributing them. If he does not have these experiences, he has not experienced the action of number, and therefore has little foundation that will help him understand the uses of mathematics.

These considerations of mathematics as acts of distribution suggest that a distribution event has at least the following components: (1) an object, or objects, or part of an object, (2) a motion. There can be no distribution unless objects are (or have been or will be) distributed. This may involve partition or duplication of objects. There must be actual or implied motion of some of the objects from their initial location to a different one.

The rational number symbols lend themselves to this model quite easily, providing we express the whole numbers as ratios. In the numeral "7," for instance, expressed as "7/1," 7 may symbolize a set of objects; 1 may symbolize a recipient set of children (one child); the diagonal line symbolizes the mutation (in this case, duplication); and the left-to-right sequence of integers (7 in the numerator and 1 in the denominator, rather than vice versa) symbolizes the direction of motion. Thus the numeral "7" symbolizes the distribution of 7 objects to 1 child. There is only 1 child involved; he acquires all 7 objects.

In the numeral "1/7," the left-to-right sequence of integers indicates that 1 object is evenly distributed to 7 children. The mutation symbolized by the diagonal line is a partition. There are 7 children, each acquires "1/7." Thus this Natural Mathematics model designates a rational number as a distribution in terms of *its outcome to each participating recipient.*

The customary pie-model for fractions also divides the pie into 7 pieces. The lesson to be learned then is what part of the pie *one* child theoretically would get if he were given one of the pieces. But in this concern with one recipient child in particular, the other six pieces are relatively de-emphasized (or regarded simply as the remainder). This orientation may overlook the fact that an actual 1/7 portion cannot be determined except insofar as there are 6 others equal to it. They may not actually be distributed, but they must exist in order for even one to be taken. However, the reason for the child to become involved in fractions, at all, is the desirability of an equitable distribution. That is, the reason for dividing a whole into sevenths, in social experience, is a situation in which such a distribution does take place. Until the child is actually interested in an equitable sharing, there is no platform for precision in any distribution.

Once this social platform exists, we suggest that the distribution model may be helpful in developing initial understanding of fractions. That is, it is appropriate for the beginning levels of the hierarchies, in which distributions arise out of problems of sharing. In later problems, involving precise measurement for cooking, construction, and record-keeping (of personal or scientific data), the more static, traditional model will shorten the process of solution. The purpose of the distribution model is to cultivate the child's development of number concepts as the result of relevant actions.

The numeral "7/1" is usually written as "7"; that is, denominators of 1 are omitted in the ordinary writing of numerals. The practice reflects a feature of simple distributions in real life: they are frequently associated with a singleton set. The purchaser of 5 cans of paint, or 1 automobile, the teacher of 30 children, the mother of 4, are all single subjects of the distribution in question. In other words, the usual denominator is 1.

Another feature of real life mirrored in the whole numbers is, of course, that a large proportion of distributions involve duplication rather than partition of the object being distributed. Heads of lettuce, apples, loaves of bread, candy bars, can be partitioned, it is true. But invariably they are first marketed in wholes. The partitioning for use may occur in a later distribution.

Objects such as automobiles, pictures, desks, are both marketed and used in wholes. So are nearly all objects which are structured for repeated use. The notion of repeatable usefulness of an object describes the kind of functionality it has. Cars are no more functional than apples; their function is only of a different nature. The function of these repeat-use objects is to serve, not nourish; to shape, but not to be part of the final construction; to transport, not to remain. Most such objects (but not all) are also internally related; that is, a variety of parts serves a variety of purposes within the total function of the object—in order that it may in fact have that function. A car contains a carburetor, a coil, a spark plug, etc., each of which serves a purpose in order that the car will eventually transport. Frequently, such parts are marketed (distributed) individually also, separate from the total which they comprise. But they themselves are then purchased in wholes. We do not buy half a carburetor any more than half a car. Persons *always* are found in wholes, as are horses, robins, and bees.

The question arises that repeat-function objects can be altered nevertheless, provided the alteration is not too great.

The top "half" of a car may be cut away, leaving everything intact except shelter. A man or animal may lose a leg or eye and yet continue to function in a sufficient number of essential ways to retain life. Philosophical interests aside, these questions have a bearing on mathematics because they pertain to what mathematics is about. If it is true that mathematics is about distributions, the differences between those objects which may be partitioned and those which may not—especially in the experience of the action—have significant implications for teaching techniques. An obvious consequence is that we should deal with fractions as partitions of objects which are partitionable, and not as symbolic resolutions of philosophical contradictions, at least with young children.

It is of interest that the distribution model accommodates improper fractions and sets of equivalent fractions immediately, at the outset of arithmetic. Consider a numeral in which the numerator is a multiple of the denominator, an "improper fraction," which is "reducible": e.g., 6/2. In the distribution model which relates the symbolic numeral to a real distribution, the numeral 6/2 symbolizes a distribution of a set of 6 over a set of 2. The best interpretation most children could give of 6/2 is that it is a division problem: 6/2 is the same as 6 divided by 2. "2 goes into 6, 3 times"; even possibly because "2 times 3 is 6."

To the young learner, the distribution model gives 6/2 *personal* meaning. Six objects are going to be distributed over 2 people, that is, to 2 people; what will *he* get? He will scarcely be interested, initially, unless he is one of the people. It is already a great social jump to be interested in the distribution if a friend is involved instead of himself. It is an even greater jump to be interested in the distribution if nobody he knows is involved. At this stage it is not likely that he will be interested in "6/2" for its own sake. But if the child has the social problem of making this distribution in such a way that he is one of the recipients, and that it is fair, he himself becomes central to the meaning. He experiences the equivalence of outcome to himself, if 3 are distributed to him directly, or 6 to 2 (him and one other), or 9 to 3 (him and two others), etc. A parallel experience is afforded by the partition distribution of 1 to 3, 2 to 6, 3 to 9, etc.

In summary, the distribution model offers a child-centered introduction to mathematics. In the early experience of the child, he is only interested in the qualitative aspects of things. His initial quantitative experiences occur in social situations in which he wishes to receive or give or share equitably. In time he learns to distribute discrete objects equitably, by matching them. The distribution model allows his initial skills and concepts to grow out of his categorization of his own behavior in these situations.

The child also encounters the problem of wishing to distribute something which is not yet prepared for matching; that is, which is not yet divided (partitioned) into discrete objects. When he does prepare these objects, his motive is still to prepare them so that they can be matched. But the preparation itself (measurement and the use of fractions) is an additional problem, and is more complex than the matching. Precise partitioning reaches a very high level of the Complexity Hierarchy.

Since the child's daily life does involve partitioning problems, nevertheless, the Media-Action and Role-Playing Hierarchies include such problems even at the initial levels. However, in these problems, the partitioning process remains rudimentary, and the emphasis is placed on the matching. The child should have many experiences requiring precision in matching before he is presented with problems requiring precision in the preparation. If he is allowed to do so, his approach to fractions and measurement will remain in the context of relevant problem-solving and will arise as a refinement of the procedures he has already internalized.

16

Mathematics as Matching

ONE-TO-ONE CORRESPONDENCE

We have said that the concrete mathematical experience is the action of distribution. Something which exists (some object) is duplicated or divided (partitioned) and moved to a new location or time. This process best becomes an "experience" to a child, when he is the recipient, and/or the distributor, of the distribution. The child could live amid distributions all his life; if they never resulted in the satisfaction of *his* needs, they are not likely to acquire meaning for him. The child may learn rote skills with numerals and yet be unable to use number, since number concepts are the result of mathematical experience.

In the move away from rote-learning of symbolic manipulations, a fruitful approach to mathematics has been the use of sets and the idea of one-to-one correspondence. The grouping of objects in sets involves the child as an active participant in setting up the distributions that eventually will take place. The grouping of objects is well within his experience; diapers and dishes are stacked; newspapers are piled; food items are roughly arranged in storage places.

"SETS": A RETROSPECTIVE CONCEPT

The initial use of groupings (sets) in mathematics education is the placement of sets in "correspondence"—one-to-one, or otherwise. Two sets are "related" or "compared." But when we use terms like these, we are looking back, from our own level of comprehension, rather than forward, from the child's. The child does not know yet what correspondence is, nor a relation, and his ideas of comparison are not in the least objective. From the child's viewpoint, he is simply given a collection of objects "here" on this side of the desk, and a collection "here" on that side of the desk, or in a picture.

MATCHING AS THE MEANS OF SOLVING PROBLEMS WITHOUT NUMBERS

Matching is the action of distributing. Matching that "comes out even" is equal distribution. Matching that "comes out even" the first time around is both equal distribution, and the criterion for equivalence. The two sets can be placed in "one-to-one correspondence." The sets are "equivalent." Their cardinal number is the same.

It should be noted that equivalent sets may be matched, ad infinitum, without necessarily arriving at the concept of "number." Number concepts are more naturally developed by the matching of non-equivalent sets. In matching equivalent sets, what is experienced by the actual matching is primarily the pairing of one with one (as implied by the one-to-one correspondence term). Even if the child places two sets of one hundred objects each, in one-to-one correspondence, he is still doing only what he was doing when he had sets of only one each. He is still matching one to one. Matching is the action of mathematics; matching can theoretically solve the problems of elementary mathematics; matching can solve these problems *without* numerals. Therefore the solution of these problems is not dependent on the use of numerals.

This is, of course, the import of the history of mathematics. As problems became more complex, their solution by matching became increasingly cumbersome, and eventually prohibitive. The development of numbers became essential for problem solution, not in theory, but in practice.

Cumulative matching is the experience symbolized by numbers. It is therefore valuable for children to have extensive practice with matching. In the end, computation will be justified mainly by the time it saves. It is therefore of equal importance that the child finally reaches a desire to save it. His initial matching experiences should be interesting, absorbing, satisfying; gradually they should become tiresome, boring, irritating. (We should remember to observe the child's reactions, more attentively than our own; we are likely to be bored much earlier than the child, when *he* is engaged in action; just as he is likely to be bored much earlier than we, when *we* are engaged in action.)

Suppose that the problem is the distribution of three candies to three children. It is solved by matching one candy to one child until the candies are gone. Each child has one. Suppose the problem is the distribution of six candies to three children. It is solved by matching one candy to one child, until the candies are gone. Each child received one and then another one, or what we symbolize as "two." The point is that neither the problem nor the solution *require* numbers at all. The problem is the distribution of sets; the solution is matching.

When we reach fractions which do not reduce to integers, the child's mathematical world need not become formidable; it can remain the same, secure problem-solving world of figuring out how to share good things. The security is the child's sure knowledge that the solution is in the activity he knows how to do—matching.

To distribute 5 candy bars to 4 children, the one-to-one matching of 5 objects to 4 children continues until each has one, and one is left. Now we must distribute 1 to 4. Mutation is necessary; the left-over candy bar must now be divided so that each child receives a piece—his fair share. These pieces are now matched with the children one-to-one. If the division were equitable, each child now has 1 and 1/4.

To distribute 4 to 5, we have a new kind of problem; there is not enough even for one time around. Someone would get left out. Again, mutation is going to be necessary. The problem is how to cut up the candy bars so that a one-to-one matching comes out even. We know that we can distribute one of them by matching pieces. To distribute one, it must be cut so that each child gets a piece. The pieces are then matched to each child (1/5). This is done for each candy bar. At the end of the last distribution, each child will have 4/5. The point is that mutation and matching, not numbers, have solved the problems. That is, the problems are genuinely solved, whether the children know anything about numbers or not.

17

Mathematical Symbolism

COUNTING AND NUMBERS

The history of counting is well known. Its impetus probably came from communication needs, in addition to the need for more efficient problem-solving. Men needed to exchange information about facts which were not practical to transport: families, animals, warriors, possessions. In this sense, numerals are language-symbols, as are words. Their unique characteristic is that they refer to quantity rather than quality.

THE DIFFERENCE BETWEEN A REPRESENTATION AND A COUNTER

We would suggest that there may be some confusion, however, between counting and the representations which preceded it. The use of fingers, stones, and even tally marks, are often referred to as early counting methods, or counters. In fact, these were *representational* matching devices, lacking the essential quality of genuine counting, namely, the use of a symbol which implies the existence of all previous symbols in a sequence. In the Theory of Sets, based on the axioms of

Zermelo-Fraenkel, this special quality of numbers corresponds to the development of a natural number as the set containing all of the preceding natural numbers, including zero. Thus $5 = \{0,1,2,3,4\}$.[1]

The point of distinction between a representation and a counter is the question whether or not an element of the representation can be distinguished from all the others, if it is considered by itself (that is, whether or not it can be used in place of all the others). A stone cannot, unless each one has a unique distinguishing feature. Even at the level of sophistication at which a large stone is used to represent five or ten smaller stones, the larger stones are not distinguishable from each other. Nor does any one of them imply the existence of any other. The same is true for tally marks.

Numerals are genuine counters. Each implies all elements of the preceding sequence. Only the terminal symbol need be used.

Word counting then remains a simple operation of matching objects to words. The terminal word connotes that particular matching *and all of the preceding ones, even if they are not spoken.* In summary, counting is the process of matching objects against a sequence of symbols, each of which is agreed to contain all previous object-symbol matchings.

The consequence of this view is that numbers are a product of counting. Counting is not an operation imposed on numbers that already exist, or that have an independent reality. Numbers are results of a sequence in time as well as space because counting itself is a sequence. Counting is a sequence of matchings, one following another. Counting is, in other words, an action.

In teaching the child to count, and to believe in the numbers which counting produces, it is of importance to distinguish between the equivalence of sets and the number of a set. Equivalence derives from matching directly, without regard to sequence or repetition. On the other hand, numbers grow out of matching cumulatively.

---

[1] Alexander Abian, *The Theory of Sets and Transfinite Arithmetic*, W. B. Saunders Co., Philadelphia, 1965.

NUMBER EXPERIENCES PRIOR TO NUMBER SYMBOLS

It is important that the child have the opportunity to develop memory of many number experiences (sequences of distributions), before he is asked to use numerals to compute. In order to assist the child in creating number images, we suggest repetitions of distributions of one to one, where the same child is the recipient of each distribution. We suggest that the child best learns the concept of "two," by being the recipient of one, and then of one again, with sufficient proximity of time that he tends to relate the two events, and remember them as sequential. And he best learns the symbol "2" by having it presented in close connection with the event-sequence.

Several factors must be considered in the amount of emphasis given to numerical symbols. Overemphasis is tempting. It is difficult to structure concrete distributions in a classroom. Consumable materials are often required. "Housekeeping" is increased. A greater difficulty is that each child must have his own personal experience. More often than not, real experiences must happen somewhat consecutively, one child after another, or in very small groups. Only rarely can a distribution be conducted by an entire classroom simultaneously. The "trading" approach is one of the few activities in which all the children can participate at the same time.

PREMATURE INTRODUCTION OF
NUMBER SYMBOLS

The point that is being made here is that all too often the pressures are toward the premature substitution of symbols for experiences. There is little danger that symbols will be introduced too late. The danger is rather that they will be emphasized too early. If the use of symbols is emphasized too early, the break between "mathematics" and experience will occur, which will alienate the child. In so doing, we begin an endless sequence of problems in the child's school-life. We place an artificial barrier in front of his real potential in mathematics; and we prevent mathematics from becoming something "of value" in the child's life. As John Dewey states:

> Mathematics is said to have disciplinary value in habituating the pupil to accuracy of statement and closeness of reasoning; it has utilitarian value in giving command of the arts of calculation involved in trade and the arts; cultural value in its enlargement of the imagination in dealing with the most general relations of things; even religious value in its concept of the infinite and allied ideas. But clearly mathematics does not accomplish such results, because it is endowed with miraculous potencies called values; it has these values if and when it accomplishes these results, and not otherwise.[2]

To summarize: In order to acquire number meanings, children must be at a twofold mental level. (1) The child must be able to remember events as well as objects; that is, he must be able to retain images of action, in a closely-connected sequence. (2) He must be able to distinguish between more or less, in relation to his own needs and satisfaction. If the child has reached this stage of maturation, he is ready to develop number ideas. If he has not, he may still be taught the name-symbols of numbers, and to count rote-style. However, this will not result in number images, but rather in language play.

We have said that the child acquires the number memory "two," by being the recipient of one, and then of one again, with a consciousness of the two events being related. He experiences the events individually and collectively. The events have meaning to him in terms of their relation to his needs. Verbal description of the events makes them more memorable. Our pedagogical problem is to ensure that the power of language is applied to, and not substituted *for*, the reality which it symbolizes.

It is our suggestion that if the child could be brought through many sequences of distributions, prior to or contiguous to counting, there would not arise the question "does he comprehend

---

[2] John Dewey, *Philosophy of Education*, Littlefield, Adams & Co., Paterson, N.J., 1961.

what he is saying"; for in this kind of experience, he is saying what he is doing; and he is doing things related to his personal interests. If counting is now taught, there is less danger of a schism between numbers and experience. The child at least has a better chance to avoid remedial work later, in an effort to relate numbers to reality, if numbers have been introduced as ways of communicating about his experience from the outset.

In the chapters on the Media-Action Hierarchy, a sequence for the child's passage from the experiences to the symbols has been suggested. The danger in the use of symbols lies not in the symbols themselves. The danger derives only from the assumption that they have any independent vitality or power which will somehow substitute itself for the child's own problem-solving action.

The numeral is a very efficient but sophisticated symbol. Between the experience and the numeral; that is, between distribution by matching and symbolic computation, a great many representations of objects and actions may be made available to the child. It is also important to have such intermediate levels of regression available. Otherwise an impasse at the symbolic level would drive the child completely back to the concrete.

18

Image Development

Concrete-to-Abstract Continuum: Objects

In the preceding chapters it has been assumed that the child enters school (or kindergarten) with a minimal vocabulary for common objects. It is *not* assumed that the child is able to use this vocabulary for solving problems, but only that he can relate the spoken word-symbol to the correct object. In a discussion of what the child has done in a trading activity with pennies and candies, for instance, it is assumed that the spoken words, "penny" and "candy," elicit appropriate images in the child's mind.

Children differ widely in their degree of development. Furthermore, image-development is a continuing process. Therefore, it is important to be aware of the sequence in which it occurs. The development proceeds from concrete to abstract, and has its foundation in experience.

THE SENSES AND CONCRETENESS

Since experience comes to the mind through the senses, it is suggested that concreteness is a function related to the number of senses which apprehend an object or experience. That is, we may think of something which may be apprehended by all the senses as more "concrete," in terms of the purely perceptual experience of the individual, than something that is apprehended by fewer of the senses. Something that can be seen, heard, felt, smelled, and tasted is thus more "concrete," in the pure sense of the word, than something which can only be seen and/or felt. At the other end of the concrete-abstract continuum are arbitrary symbols of real things or real experience.

The concrete is the tangible phenomenon which exists and can be apprehended by the senses. It is usually three dimensional and can be apprehended by many of the senses. It does not represent anything beyond itself. In this sense, it is absolutely itself. It is a particular dog, chair, house, tree, child, pebble, etc. It is not a concept in the mind of the observer, it is not an image of itself, it is not an idea of itself. It is simply present. Its concreteness can be experienced by an individual when the individual sees it, hears it, smells it, tastes it, feels it. In general it may be said that the more senses the individual uses in this perception, the more real or "present" is the object, and the more total the experience of it.

IMAGES AND MEMORY

The object is perceived by the individual through the sense avenues and then may become an internal experience which may be "re-lived." This internal "memory" or "availability" of the experience may be called an "image." Memory then becomes an "imagining" experience, a re-living of real experience, sometimes a faithful re-living, sometimes an elaborative re-living. If the latter, it is a matter of rearranging images and adding to them in order to satisfy a psychological need which was not satisfied in the original experience.

The essential point is that in order to experience images the young child must experience real objects first, and real objects must be experienced through the senses. Objects are handled, picked up, dropped, pushed, tasted, observed, smelled, heard, etc. The more senses involved, the more "known" the phenomenon.

SYMBOL AND OBJECT MATCHING

A major learning step in the normal life of the child occurs when a special arbitrary symbol is matched with the real phenomenon so that the arbitrary symbol will elicit the "image" in the mind of the child. This step is speech, in which arbitrary sounds are presented in close connection with real phenomena and experience. These arbitrary sounds may eventually be substituted for the phenomena/experience, expediting communication and learning.

When words are able to elicit images of objects, the images become objective phenomena, separated from the experiencing-event. The image has been substituted for the experience of the object, and the word mediates between the image and further learning.

SYMBOL SUBSTITUTION: A LARGE COGNITIVE LEAP

The jump from the real object to an arbitrary symbol of the real object is one of the greatest jumps an individual must make in learning. The authors maintain here that this jump can be accomplished because parents instinctively depend upon closely matching the spoken word with the real perceptual experience. The child is firmly anchored in the safety of the real perceptual experience and is required to learn only one thing—that a certain sound may be used to stand for the experience. It is a matter of "naming" the phenomenon. The child is not asked to learn a symbol for experience which he has never had, or asked to learn it separated from the experience in time and space.

The written word is a symbol of experience as is the spoken word. It is customarily taught after children have learned speech, speech being an easier mode of communication and immediately available in social situations of all kinds.

In summary, it is maintained that children are forced to take large cognitive leaps when moving from the original perceptual experiences of phenomena to representations and symbols of those phenomena. It is maintained that (1) the more complete the sensual experience of an object the easier the jump to a symbol of it, (2) the cognitive jump from the object directly to the word-symbol is made possible by use of the symbol in close connection with experience of the object, (3) there exists a theoretical continuum of representational possibilities leading from the concrete to the abstract, (4) implicit in this hierarchy is the underlying process of step by step removal of the perceptual-sensual dimensions of the real object experience.

THE REPRESENTATIONAL CONTINUUM

The steps away from reality; that is, the steps into representation, usually involve more representational distortions than we realize. A plastic model of a building, for instance, reduces size and changes construction materials; a cloth representation of a bunny removes mobility. To a child, a cloth bunny which doesn't move may be as distorted a representation as a plastic apple which is made so that it continually jumps. We take it for granted that the child will buy the illusion.

The transition from a real apple to a line drawing requires the child to (1) collapse three dimensions to two, (2) remove the color, (3) remove the smell, (4) remove the texture, (5) shrink the size, (6) place it on the page of a book and thereby remove the invitation for eating and moving it about.

This may help explain the middle-class child's superior achievement with textbooks. His parents have already assisted and encouraged him to make the personal identification with representations in place of the real (as well as with word-symbols). In reading to him, for instance, a parent will have pointed to the picture of the bunny with a reminder of the bunny they saw on the lawn, or to the picture of an apple with a reminder that there are some in the refrigerator. Such verbalized associations between representations and real objects accomplish two major assists: (1) they help the child to accept and internalize the representation; (2) they do so in a comforting, warm, enriching way. The picture of an apple becomes an extension of the real experience as well as a substitute for it.

The implication here is that whenever we present the child with a representational jump, we also do it in the same comforting, personal way, relating to a gratifying previous experience. It should be noted that a memorable experience may also have been painful. These may not be suitable for representational jumps. The child may reject them, even if they are within his capacity, for a representation is an invitation to re-live an experience.

19

The Central Role of Motivation in Natural Mathematics

In the Natural Mathematics program, motivation is considered *central* to learning, inseparable, not merely a necessary antecedent to learning. Natural Mathematics therefore provides a central place for motivation in teaching. It begins with situations which are known to be motivating and engaging to the child. If certain tangible things are motivating to a child (such as candy, toys, and money), the child should be provided with the possibility of experiencing these items in a manner consistent with his affinity for them, including the acquisition of them. Having placed priority on the motivation of the child, by providing motivating things and motivating experiences of them, National Mathematics then begins to design the possibility of an experience which allows the child to participate in the action of mathematics.

Natural Mathematics views mathematics as the conscious act of distribution. Thus experiences are designed in which the child wishes to distribute or redistribute objects. As a specific example, half the children of a group or class are provided with four pennies—the other half with four candies. Each child's problem is to acquire what he does not have and wishes to have. The action is to use what he does have to get what he does not have and wishes to have. The nature of the action is some form of matching what he has with what another child has.

Many such experiences are required before the child is able to develop not only precision in matching but social sophistication relative to the value of things and money. Skills and concepts are developed through the experiences and problems, because the teacher places priority on the latter and does not place her goals of skills and concepts in conflict with the motivational system of the child.

WHY ILLUSTRATIONS DO NOT SUBSTITUTE FOR EXPERIENCE

If, however, a teacher places priority on the learning of certain skills and concepts, and only secondarily makes a concession to the motivational system of the child, she will likely attempt to provide the child with an experience which has elements of interest to the child, as a means of illustrating skills and concepts or as a proof of them. The child's interest in such experiences will probably be far more casual, and focused only on those elements which do interest him. Frequently, these elements of interest are enticements which themselves are not central to the problem. Indeed, if the child becomes truly motivated toward these enticements, they may in fact distract him from the teacher's goals; and his "motivation" becomes a detriment to his attention to the details the teacher feels pertinent to the learning of the skills and concepts. She may then, ironically, view the child's natural motivation with apprehension and distrust, as something primitive and uncontrollable, and as a threat to concentration and attention. She will then wish to neutralize subsequent lessons by removing the irrelevant, distracting, and disturbing elements; that is, the very elements on which the child's motivation depends. Thus, when forced to place priority on skills and concepts, rather than the experiences which truly engage the child, the teacher is placed in a psychological set which may alienate her from the child and the child from learning.

ACHIEVEMENT MOTIVATION

"Achievement" motivation is the kind of motivation usually appealed to in the classroom. If it does not exist, the teacher is expected to develop it. The teacher finds herself exhorting pupils toward success in later life, whether it is ten years later in post-school life, or ten minutes later, at quiz time. She tries to convince the pupils that their effort, now, will determine their success later. She urges attention, concentration, application, and conscientiousness. If motivation exists, but not in the direction of the material to be learned, or if the concept of success which the child holds differs from the socially acceptable, the teacher finds herself attempting to modify the child's goals. That is, she tries to redirect the motivation.

These are the activities of teachers which exhaust their patience and energy, depress their enthusiasm, and induce feelings of hopelessness and all of the consequent defenses. The first prerequisite to being a good teacher is to survive as a teacher at all. Occasionally, a teacher of tremendous innate vitality achieves a large measure of success through sheer force of personality. These are the teachers whom children may remember, sometimes all their lives, sometimes with affection, sometimes not. Without devaluing the importance of teacher-personality, the primary roles in education are held by the child and his environment, of which the teacher is a part.

Achievement motivation is natural if it is a result of successful social and problem-solving experiences. In this sense, Natural Mathematics views "achievement" motivation as a consequence of education, as well as a means. The motivation directly available as a means is the tendency for children to act in response to immediate interests and goals.

ACTION AND NATURAL MOTIVATION

In Natural Mathematics, motivation is viewed as the child's willingness to act. Children want to move, or do things. They may want to move, simply for the sake of movement. Free movement is in itself pleasant, "motivating" for its own sake. It does not imply causality, neither a prior reason nor a later consequence. Movement, however, may *discover* goals and gradually may become more and more goal-directed.

If we wish to align our efforts to natural energy, then, we will encourage and not inhibit movement. The Greek philosophers and mathematicians are remembered for their strolling study habits as well as their thoughts. We ourselves pace the floor. Many of us acquire all kinds of nervous activities, such as foot tapping, when our circumstances inhibit our action-drive. Pupils who drum on their desks, chew their pencils, twist their hair, or constantly shift in their seats, may be doing their best to reconcile their action-drive with their school environment. When we require pupils to remain at desks, we may turn a natural motivation into an enemy. If we maintain that pupils can only really learn if they are immobile, we are maintaining that learning accompanies only unnatural behavior. The truth is that the natural modes of learning are often disturbing and disquieting to adults, because current programs have not integrated action with academics.

The authors have suggested that mathematics, which is concerned with distributions, be viewed as an action. It is of course not implied that mathematics per se is an action, but that it is experienced as an action. Mathematics, like running, becomes an action when someone does it. The action resides in the actor.

Mathematics, by its nature, should be motivating to children; however, usually it is not. Both pupils and elementary teachers often find it the most difficult, least interesting of all of the subject areas. We suggest that this is likely a consequence of premature emphasis on conceptualization, a premature departure from matching, a premature stress on computation. Action, which is at the heart of mathematics, is removed from it before it has really been experienced.

The removal of this action is likely to be detrimental to all children, but particularly to the culturally disadvantaged. We have suggested that "achievement" motivation is learned, a product of education. The culturally disadvantaged child begins school at a distinct disadvantage motivationally. He is not confident of deferred gratifications; his motivations are more confined to those which are unconscious and direct. His innate tendency to act has not been modified by cultural experiences which would encourage a tendency to wait. If we remove action from mathematics for this child, we sever its connections even more radically.

Prior to the development of role-playing, observation of activity will find very unreliable motivation. If the child is able to control most or all of the action, it is likely to be more motivating than if he is forced to be a passive observer and required to report on the action; or even if he is allowed to be an active participant, but only as a receiver of the action. Children often ask and demand, "Let me do it."

CONVERGENT VERSUS DIVERGENT

The difference between convergent and divergent teaching techniques is clearly evident in our response to this natural and spontaneous motivation. The convergent technique will not permit the child to do it, until he has been taught how to do it by some other means than doing it. It will make sure that when he does it, he does it correctly. It will make the "doing" an illustration of a known "how." The divergent technique, on the other hand, will accede to the request, "Let me do it"; it will expect errors, new starts, unexpected approaches, and tangents. The divergent technique will take more time and more planning at the outset. But it will have two enormous advantages in terms of educational goals. The child's independence, resourcefulness, and ingenuity will have been nourished; and his experiences will have constituted lasting learning, because they were his own. He will be more willing to proceed to new learning, and he will be more capable of proceeding.

CHILD AS DIRECTOR

Being a director of action, as well as participant, is most motivating. It assures the child of his identification as part of the action, and of his centrality in the action. In mathematics, being a participant in a distribution requires being distributor or recipient, or both. Many studies indicate that the disadvantaged child is likely to feel less in control of external happenings than the middle-class child. That is, the locus of control is often external to the disadvantaged and internal to the middle-class child. Since the solving of problems requires the solver to act upon internal intuition, it is necessary to allow the disadvantaged child many opportunities to be the prime mover in solving distribution problems. This may be achieved more successfully if the child is allowed to become a part of an actual problem in the real world, in which he is allowed to distribute the elements physically.

In summary:

Children like to manipulate things, tangible things. Natural Mathematics begins with the distribution and redistribution of tangible things.

Children like to explore. In Natural Mathematics, children do explore, take many paths, make many choices.

Children like to have experiences of control. In Natural Mathematics, they may.

Children want to solve their own problems. In Natural Mathematics, they are given the opportunity.

For the culturally disadvantaged, we suggest that extensive experiences of Natural Mathematics will help to overcome the deficits in their pre-school experiences.

REWARDS

The usefulness of rewards in learning is manifest, but easily abused. Rewards are motivating. It has been postulated that there exists a hierarchy of rewards beginning with tangible rewards for the less mature child; then social approval for the more mature child; and finally achievement for its own sake. Many studies show that disadvantaged children are lower on this reinforcement hierarchy than the "achievement" motivated middle-class child. This has often been the rationale for emphasizing tangible, concrete rewards for this type of child.

Extrinsic rewards

The authors are not convinced that emphasis on rewards, extrinsic to the learning action, is the most effective teaching policy. It may motivate and train, admittedly, but possibly at the expense of the full potentials of an education. Education is an on-going process. Means, being used toward a tentative end, should be allowed to alter the end. As Dewey would say, we must be able to "learn as we go along." What we learn may change our entire direction. This is the essence of the divergent approach. An extrinsic reward, on the other hand, may make our end inflexible. If we change our direction, we may sacrifice the reward, because it is generally tied in with a specific, convergent goal or outcome.

An end, in this on-going process, should become a new means. If it does not, learning stops; it does not become self-generating. An extrinsic reward may not become a new means. It may be an interruption, even a termination, of the learning process. Reactivation then may require the offering of a new reward.

Intrinsic rewards

It seems that it is preferable, educationally, that the reward be built into the activity. A professed ultimate goal of education is that the pupil should be better able to solve his problems. "Knowledge" is often taught because we judge it to be useful in this purpose. But we may never be able to induce the child to *use* knowledge, until we have allowed him to experience its development in connection with his own problem-solving. Thus, if children solve problems in which their rewards are a *part* of the problem, they will be more likely to regard the action of solving problems as a rewarding experience itself, than if the rewards are arbitrary, artificial, and unrelated to the action.

The disadvantaged child is less able to delay gratification. Within his experience there are fewer opportunities for delayed gratification, and when offered, they are often unreliable. For this child, motivation by promised reward can produce anxiety rather than effort. For this child, even more than others, the experience itself should be reinforcing. The distribution of tangible, desired objects, and money which symbolizes desired things, should characterize many of the activities of the disadvantaged child.

All of this is not to say that there is an exclusive formula for motivating a child or a group of children. Motivation is complex, and depends as well upon many general social and psychological influences in the classroom: the general climate, the relationship with the teacher, the relationships among the children, experiences which immediately precede the particular experience for which motivation is desired, etc. Within this framework, Natural Mathematics provides a program of *problem-solving* activities which are also motivating, and which relate academics to solutions which the child seeks as valuable for himself.

20

Natural Mathematics Encourages Divergent Thinking

The "divergent approach" challenges the child to look for a variety of things which can be done with his material, or a variety of ways to solve a problem, or a variety of consequences to a given problem. "Divergent teaching" searches for situations in which diverse approaches are appropriate.

The divergent approach is probably more difficult to use in mathematics than in social studies or language arts. We have been conditioned to the view that mathematics is an exact science, or a logical sequential structure. We may therefore be somewhat prejudiced against the child's view that mathematics begins as a method of obtaining equity of distribution in social interactions.

TRIAL AND ERROR

The divergent approach not only tolerates but encourages guesses, blind alleys, and unsuccessful trials. It frees the child to truly discover. We may remain certain that what he discovers will be eventually the logically consistent structure which we believe mathematics to be; but its internal consistency cannot be perceived by the child who has never had a chance to experience the results of inconsistent systems. Learning is essentially a matter of making contrasts. Therefore, we question the protective policy of guiding the child always to the correct discovery. This usually is not discovery at all. A presentation of examples of a general concept, presented before the statement of the general concept, has already discovered the concept. From the learner's point of view, the real discovery is to discover what the teacher had in mind. For true discovery, the wrong concepts are as important as the right ones; the mistaken conclusions are as important as the correct ones.

We are already trapped when we concentrate on concepts as goals. Our primary educational concern is the process by which concepts are developed and assimilated. Our task is to provide the maximum opportunity for this process to take place. Our emphasis in teaching the "correct" concepts, in this sense, reflects our lack of confidence in human learning outcomes. For if we believe that the natural learning process can eventually lead to incorrect concepts, even after the child has had a rich and unbiased opportunity to develop valid concepts, we are questioning the philosophical justification of "education" as superior to arbitrary conditioning.

DANGERS OF GUIDED DISCOVERY

Of course, our drive to "bring the learner" to valid concepts as quickly as possible is a good drive as far as our ethics are concerned. We want the child to be able to advance as quickly as possible, to score well in standardized achievement tests, to experience academic success. But these drives on our part do not guarantee good educational techniques. Our haste in fact may impede the child's progress. Our directiveness may limit his intellectual creativity. Our insistence on the shortest route deprives him of all the scenery which would motivate him to travel further. When we "correct" the child's discovery of whatever he discovers, it may decrease the security of his learning platform. It may threaten his confidence and elicit the defense mechanism of hostility toward the subject matter. It may encourage him to adopt the attitude that the subject matter is indeed an artificial exercise imposed on him for artificial purposes. The pupil may forgive us personally, but he may not forgive the process of inquiry which led him into this embarrassment.

In other words, it may be preferable to permit an incorrect discovery to stand, until additional experience leads the child to correct it himself, than to reject his discovery in the name of "quick" learning. What is really educatively important is the child's engagement and satisfaction in the *process* of learning. If this is nourished, the outcomes will correct themselves. If it is neglected or suppressed, the child's learning potential is sacrificed. We would do better to use our own concepts simply to set an additional experience in motion, and our skills to keep it in motion, and to have less concern with the direction it takes or the concepts that result from it. If it is an experience of interest to the child, if it involves a problem near his level of security but with possibilities beyond, we may feel confident that learning will result. If it is not the learning we had in mind, the experience should not therefore be considered educationally unsuccessful. Genuine learning can always be restructured; genuine learning, in fact, is constantly restructured. It is the superimposed learning which remains rigid, untransferable and unfruitful.

ILLUSTRATION OF DIVERGENT PROBLEM-SOLVING THROUGH NATURAL MATHEMATICS

Certain criteria have been suggested for the effective introduction of the young child to mathematics; and especially the young disadvantaged child. These include:

1. Introduction of mathematics as a medium of social interaction through the process of distribution.
2. Initiation of mathematics at the concrete level, that is, in the distribution of "real" objects in which such objects are physically distributed.

3. The integration of mathematical skills and concepts within the problem-solving process itself, that is, the non-separation of the skills and concepts from the problem's action.
4. The design of problems in which the rewards, at least in the fundamental stages of mathematical learning, are intrinsic to the problem.

Each of these criteria is permissive of divergent problem-solving processes. As an illustration of teaching which allows divergent thinking and problem-solving, we may review the Natural Mathematics activity in which each child in a class is presented with a bag containing four pennies or four candies. The teacher gives no directives except that the children are free to do with their bags and their contents whatever they decide.

The initial technique demonstrated here is one of problem development. At this level, the teacher does not devise a problem which she then must justify to the children as being of possible interest. She presents them, rather, with materials from which each child may generate his own problem. For each child who decides that either more candies or more pennies would better satisfy his personal needs or wishes, a number of appraisals and choices present themselves: to what extent does he want to alter the distribution; can he find a child who wishes to make a compatible exchange; is a one-to-one matching equitable, or two-to-one, or one-to-four; how do the other children's exchanges affect his evaluation; is there an advantage in deferring his decision; is he able to retract or rectify exchanges at the close of the trading period; has he accomplished his objectives; how will he alter his solution process when the activity is repeated?

Comparing this activity against the criteria mentioned above, it can be seen that the substance of the activity was redistribution within a context of direct social interaction; that the distribution was concrete, depending neither on representations nor symbols; that the mathematical processes involved were not separate skills used as "means" to solve the various problems, but rather the actual activities of the child; that the learning intended by the presentation of the materials was not rigidly confined, nor was each child directed to learn the same thing (ready or not, interested or not, able or not). There was no "correct" solution or "correct" answer. Indeed, there was no "correct" problem. There were only actual solutions and actual answers to whatever problem actually existed. The reward was embedded in the adequacy of the solution to the child, and it consisted of the same tangible materials from which his problem generated. Furthermore, no child finished with the indirect penalty of no reward. Even unsatisfactory solutions leave him a part of his original material.

The divergence of behavior, however, does not preclude learning from taking place; it only does not force it to be identical for all children at the same time. It therefore, in fact, *allows* learning instead of restricting it. Consider the learning which takes place in the activity: depending on the child's own progression, he engages in matching, counting, adding, subtracting; his value judgments involve ratios, quantitative equity, equivalence; his decisions involve planning, foresight, analysis, choice, evaluation. In reference to the quality of learning, in terms of assimilation and transferability, we can be assured that internalization is at a maximum, since nothing external to the child's interest and purpose is offered.

We perhaps still retain a sense of anxiety about our "failure" to identify the precise learning goal for each child beforehand. We may feel that good teaching does pre-identify specific goals, and that to this extent, good teaching must be convergent. The prescription of goals, however, if it is to remain child-centered, must remain tentative. They may suggest the kind of learning experience to set in motion, but they may not restrict its outcome. Otherwise, the goals become teacher-centered. The consolation which teachers seek from "at least knowing what they wanted to teach, and knowing that they gave a good, clear explanation of it," does not really assuage their frustration that many of the children did not learn it. It is hoped that the child-centered approach, that is, the approach which is natural to the child, will help both child and teacher to collaborate in more successful learning.

21

Natural Mathematics:
A Universal Model

THE TECHNIQUES ARE NOT CONFINED
TO MATHEMATICS

The proposals presented in this book have suggested substantial changes in the mathematics teaching procedures for the young child, and especially for the young disadvantaged child. However, the proposed approach is confined neither to mathematics nor to the disadvantaged. The central principle of the approach is that it is child-centered rather than subject-centered. This principle should apply to the teaching of any subject and the teaching of any child.

It has been stated explicitly that mathematical concepts grow out of the child's natural experiences, as he observes his own behavior and categorizes it. Social concepts also grow out of his natural experiences, as he observes his own behavior and categorizes it. Isolated social skills are as useless as isolated mathematical skills. Therefore, social studies teaching is subject to the same criteria: does it grow out of a problem which is real to the child; does it involve genuine social intercourse; does he operate initially with real things and real actions; is he introduced to hypothetical problems sequentially; is his mode of solving social problems graduated from concrete to abstract?

In Chapters 7 and 8, this approach to reading was specifically suggested. It will be recalled that the child's introduction to reading (by word-card selection) involved *choice*. Choice is the primary criterion of a real problem. If the child does not have to make a choice, no problem exists.

The same criteria also apply to science. Skills and concepts of science grow out of a child's natural problem-solving experiences. The ultimate goal of science is not the compilation of isolated information, but rather the development of the scientific method for the investigation of natural phenomena.

THE TECHNIQUES ARE NOT CONFINED
TO THE DISADVANTAGED

As stated in the Overview in Chapter 1, the program of Natural Mathematics, in its developmental emphasis, is designed for the teaching of all children. It is especially needed by the disadvantaged, not because the disadvantaged have a different "learning style," but because they are in an earlier developmental stage when they come to school. It is generally thought that children in Headstart classes gain because of increased "cultural exposure." However, these are often the same children who have been "exposed to the culture" since infancy through TV. What they have lacked is not observation of "the culture," but participation in it. They have seen it operate, but they have not had a chance to direct it. This is not to say they have not had their chances to direct the events in their *own* culture. They learn when to run, when to fight, how to get attention. What they lack is the developmental progression which would result in the readiness for "school achievement."

This is the situation of *every* young child at some time in his early years. The difference is that most middle-class children are brought through it by educational experiences provided by their parents—both deliberately and incidentally because of family practices—before they ever come to school. The deprived child, on the other hand, is not brought through it. He comes to school without it. This is one of the meanings of deprivation. And unless the school program provides for this development, this child will probably not become a successful student. There are many middle-class children, also, who are "culturally deprived" in this respect. Most teachers have several in the classroom. These children will gain equally from a teaching technique which provides them with a developmental foundation.

REMEDIAL ADAPTATIONS

Phase III of the Media-Action Hierarchy has been referred to as a specially effective level for remedial work in mathematics in particular. This is the level in which problems are solved by drawing the elements and using drawing also to represent the action. Theoretically, many of the older children in need of remedial work ought to be regressed all the way to Phase I, on the Role-Playing Hierarchy as well as the Media-Action Hierarchy. This extreme regression is acceptable to the younger child, but becomes less acceptable as the child becomes more mature and more self-conscious. Classroom materials in Phase I are the real objects. The young child is delighted with pennies, candies, and small toys. The adolescent is embarrassed. There are undoubtedly more sophisticated objects at reasonable cost, but the choice is restricted. Furthermore, the adolescent or young adult is only too aware of his placement in a remedial program. He often is sensitive and defensive in attitude. This attitude prevents him from allowing himself to engage wholeheartedly in the problem-solving, and may not allow either media or actions to be psychologically real to him.

Many children's failure to internalize mathematics does not become apparent until after one or two years in school. They learn to count, they can do simple sums and subtractions, they even can understand the demonstration of a simple word problem. As illustrated in the Teacher's Story in the Prologue, it is only when they reach a level at which independent conceptual thought is necessary, that it becomes apparent they are unprepared. This is not because they have been taught by rote or without conceptual explanations. It is because conceptual explanations have been emphasized to a greater extent than the personal experiences from which concepts develop.

The primary criterion of Natural Mathematics is that it remain child-centered. Adherence to this criterion requires the educator to place primary emphasis on the child's view. Similarly, the educator must accede to the child's view about remedial activities. If the child is unable to participate in a remedial activity, then for that child the activity is not, in fact, remedial. The authors have found that Phases III and IV on the Media-Action Hierarchy, when combined with Phase V, offer a range of compromise that often is both acceptable and effective. The pupil may also be allowed to regress to Phase III of the Role-Playing Hierarchy, that is, to problems to which he can relate closely, even though they are not actually his own. The remedial pupil's objection to picture-drawing (as babyish, time consuming, and unnecessary) is largely met by his own inability to solve the problem strictly symbolically. The teacher is thus allowed to say, "If you can solve the problem without it, skip it." The child who has been brought along the Media-Action Hierarchy, of course, has no such resentments about regressing to earlier levels for tough problems or new kinds of elements or actions.

It is better to employ correct developmental techniques in a child's early education than to let the difficulties arise and then remedy them later. However, more than a third of the nation's children are already in these difficulties. These are the children who constitute the present crisis in education.

A CLOSING WORD TO THE TEACHER

The authors appreciate the substantial differences in the conduct of a class engaged in either "old" or "new" mathematics compared to a class engaged in Natural Mathematics. In the early Phases, the pupils are in physical action. They are often moving around the room. They are talking, sometimes arguing. If the events are real, their outcome cannot always be predicted. However, the authors have found that the trading procedure used with small children tends to engage the withdrawn child with other children and neutralize the aggressive behavior of the acting-out child. The children soon learn to cooperate with one another within the rules of the activity. Although they are moving and active, the activity is purposeful and provides a reference for learning social behavior, as well as academics.

The authors are not recommending a laissez-faire distortion of Dewey's philosophy of education. It will be recalled that a great many educators misinterpreted Dewey's principles to mean, "the children should be allowed to do anything they want." This kind of passive resignation relieves the teacher of responsibility. The authors' program, on the other hand, places responsibility *on* the teacher to see that the children are, in fact, engaged in educational activities, and calls on her flexibility in allowing the children to be divergent *within* these activities.

We encourage the teacher to try Natural Mathematics. It will be of help to the child if the teacher can incorporate any part of it. A child in learning difficulty on all of the hierarchies will be assisted by a regression on any one of them. A child who needs extensive experience in a certain phase will be helped by even a few such experiences. It is thus the authors' hope that the teacher will use this approach and these techniques to whatever degree may be permitted by his teaching circumstances and his convictions.

Index

37353

Dwyer

Teaching children through natural mathematics

DATE DUE

APR 19 '72			
OCT 3 0 1973			

GAYLORD   PRINTED IN U.S A